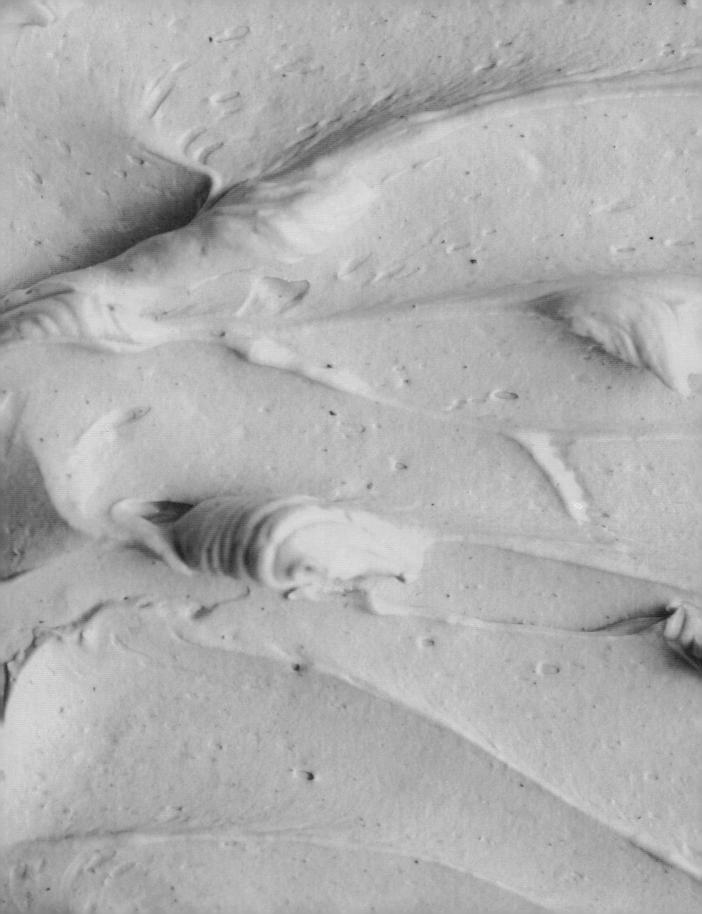

BAKE
AUSTRALIA
GREAT

THIS BOOK WAS WRITTEN ON THE
LANDS OF THE GADIGAL PEOPLE OF
THE EORA NATION. WE ACKNOWLEDGE
AND PAY OUR RESPECTS TO THEIR
ELDERS — PAST, PRESENT AND FUTURE.

BAKE AUSTRALIA GREAT

KATHERINE SABBATH

murdoch books
Sydney | London

CONTENTS

GO AHEAD: BAKE MY DAY!

CHAPTER 1

EASY AS...

CHAPTER 2

SHE'LL BE RIGHT

GO AHEAD: BAKE MY DAY!

Tie on your apron, preheat your oven and grease your cake tins, because we're here to bake our great country even greater. Australia has a rich culinary landscape, reflecting a wide selection of traditional foods and recipes, unique treats, much-loved cultural imports from many different lands, iconic sights and sites — and this cookbook is my celebration of it all.

Here are our beloved national icons — both natural and man-made — whipped up from all our favourite flavours and ingredients (including large amounts of buttercream!). Great baking, after all, is at the core of our Australian national heritage. Our First Nations Australians were the world's first bakers. In 2016 archaeologists found evidence for this at Cuddie Springs in northern New South Wales, in the shape of an ancient grinding stone that had been used to reduce grass seeds to flour. This has been dated as around 36,000 years old — evidence that Aboriginal people were grinding seeds some 20,000 years before those fly-by-night ancient Egyptians started showing off by baking loaves in the shape of a Sphinx. This historical fact should fill the heart of every Australian with pride and joy — we truly are the spiritual home of the cupcake.

My German grandmother, Liselotte, taught me to bake (and, most importantly, to bake with love) when I was a little girl. At 14, double chocolate brownies and caramel slice were my faves. I was a tad shy, so baking exciting treats for my friends and family was a good way to show I loved them without having to actually speak.

I like to think of myself as being a mixing bowl of Australian cultural imports and traditions. My mother, Yen, is Vietnamese–Australian and came here at 16 as a refugee after the Vietnam War. She's been a social worker for over 20 years and she cries whenever she comes to one of my cake demonstrations! My father, Hans, is an Australian whose German parents settled here after the Second World War. He is a SUPER-handy man and can fix absolutely anything. He gave me my eye for detail and also my very first cake smoother: a Gyprock scraper from his toolbox. We love going to the hardware store together.

I started working life as a high-school Geography, History and English teacher and my students have always been my best taste-testers and biggest supporters. They convinced me I should give up teaching (thanks, guys: was it the homework?) to make cakes instead. I've been living the 'cake life' professionally now since 2015.

I live with my husband Simon (graphic designer and cyclist, who claims to be extremely savoury-toothed, but secretly LOVES eating left-over cake tops) and Pluto, our Manchester terrier, who helps me burn off the excess sugar by running me around the park.

This book is to help us celebrate all that is great about Australian baking. It has been conceptualised, designed and taste-tested (repeatedly, by the savoury-toothed cyclist) right here in Sydney, Australia. It's designed to be your best mate in the kitchen with easy-to-follow recipes, loads of tips and tricks to make your next masterpiece easier, and recipe ideas to suit all tastes.

So, if you're inspired to whip up an Edible Outback Terrarium for the family, engineer an elegant Sydney Opera House Pav for morning tea at work, or celebrate a special birthday with an iconic heritage Big Pineapple cake, get out your wooden spoon and get started.

KEEPING YOUR COOL IN THE KITCHEN: MY TIPS AND TRICKS

I've always believed that home baking should be gratifying and delicious, but above all else, it should be enjoyable. If you're feeling the pressure and 'heat' of the kitchen, simple missteps can compound into bigger problems and a not-so-pleasant baking experience. Here are my nifty tips for no-fuss, enjoyable baking.

1. BE PREPARED

Make a list of what you need before you start to guarantee that everything is on hand and you won't need to make a last-minute dash to the supermarket (in your pyjamas). If your recipe involves multiple steps such as baking, frosting and decorating, a timeline can be a really useful tool. This will ensure you've given yourself enough time to complete each step and that, most importantly, it's ready when your buddies arrive!

2. TAKE INSPIRATION

Some of my most interesting cakes have been inspired by my favourite things, such as Australian icons, art, architecture and the exciting bits and bobs that I find in the confectionery aisle of my local supermarket. Feel free to use whatever you have in the cupboard to create your next masterpiece, whether it's left-over sprinkles, chunks of honeycomb, chopped up jersey caramels or colourful meringues (these look awesome when crushed!). Grouping decorations in interesting colour combinations is a really striking way to style a cake.

3. USE CAKE FLOUR

Cake flour is lower in protein than regular flour, so you're less likely to over-mix the cake batter. It also gives a much more delicate and fluffy texture (although the cakes will work just fine if you choose to use regular flour). Cake flour is available in some supermarkets and specialty grocers, or you can make your own version:

- For 3 cups (480 g) of all-purpose/plain cake flour, sift 2⅔ cups (430 g) plain flour with ⅓ cup (50 g) cornflour.

- For 3 cups (480 g) of self-raising cake flour, sift 1½ tablespoons of baking powder with the all-purpose cake flour.

4. BE MINDFUL OF TEMPERATURE

I've specified that most of the refrigerated ingredients are to be used at room temperature. I find that when all the ingredients are close to the same temperature, they mix together easily and evenly, and produce a more uniform texture.

5. CHEAT IF YOU HAVE TO!

If you would like to make a three-layer cake but prefer not to have to worry about levelling your cakes, simply pour the batter evenly into three cake tins and bake until the layers bounce back when gently pressed. Alternatively, you can invest in a cake levelling tool, which will do the work of neatly slicing your cake layers for you.

If you're really struggling with the cake baking experience, don't be afraid to use packet mix cakes — that's where I started when I was in primary school and I continued using them well into my teens. Some of the cheaper brands can taste overly sweet and 'fake', but they certainly played a role in igniting my passion for baking.

6. CHECK YOUR CAKE

All the temperatures given in my recipes are for a fan-forced oven; I find that this gives the best results. However, not all ovens are created equal and you can end up with lopsided, domed or uneven cakes. Placing your cake in the centre of the oven will allow for even airflow and ultimately more even cooking. For an even more level cake, it's worth rotating your cake halfway around, two-thirds of the way through the cooking time. You can even buy 'bake even' strips to ensure even baking results, or make your own by soaking wet strips of towel in cold water and wrapping these in foil to form an insulated collar around the outside of the cake tin.

7. CHILL OUT AND FREEZE

Fridges and freezers are often under-utilised when it comes to home baking. I like to avoid waste and make the best use of my time by storing cakes, Swiss meringue buttercream, cheesecake fillings, salted caramel and chocolate ganache in the fridge or freezer for later use.

Most cakes can be baked and refrigerated for up to about 4 days, and frozen for up to 2 months (mudcakes can last up to 3 months). Wrap each cake in a double layer of plastic wrap. Most cakes may be left at room temperature overnight, but chilling them in the refrigerator will make them easier to cut and stack.

Buttercream can be made in advance and stored in the refrigerator for up to about 10 days. Salted caramel and ganache can both be kept in the fridge for a couple of weeks, but will need to be reheated before use.

Be sure to allow sufficient time to let chilled cakes return to room temperature before serving — nobody wants a mouthful of solid buttercream or hardened ganache!

8. PRACTISE!

As with any skill, when it comes to cake baking and decorating, practice makes perfect. The more you bake (and the more mistakes you make), the more opportunities you will have to learn. Every baker has had their fair share of kitchen disasters (I plead horribly guilty to all charges), but once you've picked yourself up and wiped up the mess, you're not likely to make the same mistake again.

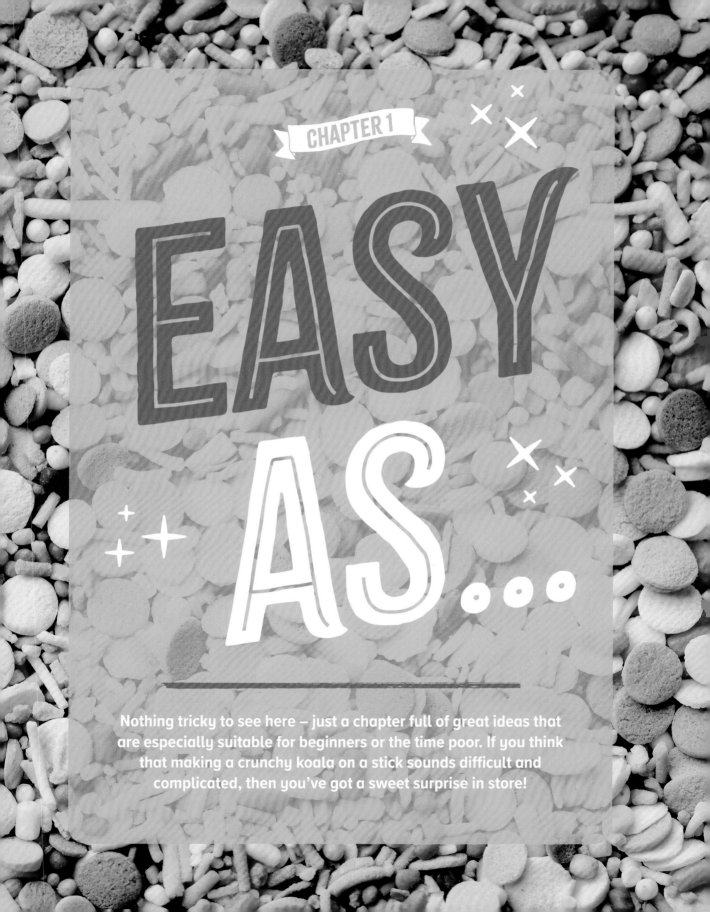

CHAPTER 1

EASY AS...

Nothing tricky to see here — just a chapter full of great ideas that are especially suitable for beginners or the time poor. If you think that making a crunchy koala on a stick sounds difficult and complicated, then you've got a sweet surprise in store!

SURF'S UP COOKIES

Surfing is like a religion Down Under, and tie-dyed singlets and boardies – those oh-so-subtle fashion statements – can be spotted at every beach. These (tough) cookies will withstand the testing Aussie heat, making them the perfect gnarly treat at any beach party or summer picnic. Be sure to bake extra – all the wave enthusiasts will be frothin' for a bite!

MAKES 12

SUGAR COOKIES

1½ cups (240 g) plain flour, sifted
½ teaspoon salt
100 g (3½ oz) unsalted butter, softened
½ cup (110 g) caster sugar
1 egg, chilled
1 teaspoon vanilla extract or vanilla bean paste

1. Sift the flour and salt into a large bowl.

2. Using an electric mixer fitted with the paddle attachment, cream the butter and sugar until fluffy and pale. Beat in the egg.

3. Add the flour mixture and mix on low speed until thoroughly combined. Mix in the vanilla.

4. Form the dough into a ball and place on a large piece of plastic wrap. Wrap the sides of the plastic over the ball, then press down with the palm of your hand to make a disc about 2.5 cm (1 inch) thick. Finish wrapping the disc with the plastic. Chill the dough for about 30 minutes.

5. Unwrap the dough, place on a large piece of baking paper or silicone mat and roll out until 5 mm (¼ inch) thick. Slide the baking paper or mat and dough onto a board, then refrigerate for about 15 minutes.

6. Preheat the oven to 160°C (320°F) fan forced. Line two baking trays with baking paper or silicone baking mats.

7. Cut the chilled dough into shapes using cookie cutters or make paper templates to cut around. Place the shapes on the lined trays, leaving 2.5 cm (1 inch) clearance around each one. Reserve any excess dough.

8. Put the trays of cookies in the freezer for 15 minutes. Transfer the trays to the oven and bake the cookies for 12–15 minutes or until the edges are slightly golden. Leave the trays on wire racks to cool for 15 minutes, then gently remove the cookies to finish cooling.

9. Repeat the rolling, cutting and baking with the remaining cookie dough.

ROYAL ICING

2 cups (280 g) icing (confectioners')
    sugar, sifted
20 g (¾ oz) egg white powder
½ teaspoon lemon juice
¼ cup (60 ml) water
Gel food colouring of your choice
    (see tip)

1. Add the icing sugar, egg white powder and lemon juice to the clean mixer bowl. Using the paddle attachment, mix on low speed for 10 minutes.

2. Stir in the water in small increments (1 teaspoon at a time) until the icing reaches a '10-second' consistency, meaning when you run the tip of a knife through the icing, the line disappears after 10 seconds. This gives the ideal consistency for outlining and filling the cookies.

3. Divide the icing into bowls and tint with gel food colouring as desired. Keep the icing covered with plastic wrap at all times.

DECORATION

1. Put each different colour of icing in a separate piping bag so it is no more than two-thirds full and secure with an elastic band. Use scissors to cut off the tip of each bag. Keep the tips tucked into a damp cloth when not in use.

2. Pipe an outline on each cookie with one colour of icing and then pipe inside the outline with the different colours of icing until you reach the centre. Pull a toothpick through the colours to create a tie-dyed effect. If needed, use a clean toothpick to gently connect the icing over any missing spots.

3. Allow the icing to dry for at least 12 hours before packaging the cookies.

STORAGE

- The cookies can be stored in an airtight container at room temperature for up to 2 weeks. They can also be frozen.
- The icing can be stored for up to 3 days. Refrigerate it in a bowl with a damp cloth and plate placed on top.

Decorating Tip

- I used electric pink, electric orange, electric green, electric blue and electric yellow gel food colouring to decorate the cookies.

FAIRY BREAD CAKE

When I was growing up, no kid's birthday could be celebrated without a plate of sugar-studded, floppy white fairy bread (and hold the butter please, we're in margarine territory). I'm pretty sure I learned on the first day of primary school that 'one simply does not party without sprinkle-covered bread'. You'll be delighted with this fluffier and rather less floppy version of my childhood favourite. Cake cheekily masquerading as non-cake is among my favourite things in life, right up there with miniature fruit and vegetables, and dogs wearing T-shirts.

SERVES 12

VANILLA CAKE

1 cup (250 g) unsalted butter, softened
1½ cups (330 g) caster sugar
2 teaspoons vanilla extract
4 eggs, at room temperature
1 large pinch salt
3 cups (480 g) self-raising flour
1 cup (250 ml) milk, at room temperature

1. Preheat the oven to 160°C (320°F) fan forced. Grease a 25.5 cm (10 inch) square cake tin and line the tin with baking paper.
2. Using an electric mixer, cream the butter, sugar and vanilla until light and fluffy. Add the eggs, one at a time, beating until combined. Add the salt.
3. Alternately fold in the flour and the milk, in one-third increments. Fold until just combined.
4. Pour the batter into the tin. Bake for about 40 minutes or until a skewer inserted into the centre of the cake comes out clean. Cool in the tin for 30 minutes, then turn out onto a wire rack to cool completely.

CREAM CHEESE FROSTING

250 g (9 oz) cream cheese, softened
2½ tablespoons single (pure) cream
½ teaspoon lemon juice (optional)

1. Using an electric mixer, beat the cream cheese, cream and lemon juice, if using, until thick and creamy.

ASSEMBLY AND DECORATION

¾ cup (135 g) assorted sprinkles

1. Use a long, thin knife to level the top of the cake.
2. Spread the cream cheese frosting over the cake and cover with sprinkles.
3. Cut the cake into large triangles or serve as one giant slice.

FANTALES®
FUDGE COOKIES

There are very few things in life as comforting as a freshly baked cookie, toasty warm from the oven. Now what if that wholesome cookie were filled with a molten, fudgy, chocolatey centre, courtesy of your favourite childhood caramel? If that sounds irresistible, almost show-offy — well, it is! You can stuff each cookie with one Fantales, or you can stuff them with three — no judgement from me! Just be sure to serve these with a glass of milk (even hot Milo®, if you're feeling dangerous) and a snuggly blanket.

MAKES 20

¾ cup (180 g) unsalted butter, softened
¾ cup (165 g) caster sugar
½ cup (80 g) dark brown sugar
1 teaspoon vanilla bean paste
1 egg, chilled
2⅓ cups (375 g) plain flour
1½ teaspoons salt
1 cup (190 g) dark chocolate chips
20 Fantales

1. Preheat the oven to 160°C (320°F) fan forced. Line two baking trays with baking paper.

2. Using an electric mixer fitted with the paddle attachment, beat the butter, caster sugar and brown sugar for 5 minutes or until light and fluffy.

3. Add the vanilla and egg and beat until well combined. Add the flour and salt and beat until just combined. Add the chocolate chips and beat until incorporated. Refrigerate the cookie dough for at least 30 minutes so that it firms up and is easier to handle.

4. Roll the dough into balls the size of a golf ball. Press one Fantales into the middle of each ball of dough, ensuring it is completely covered. Place on the trays, leaving 2.5 cm (1 inch) clearance around each one.

5. Working in batches, bake the cookies for 20 minutes or just until golden. Cool on a wire rack or enjoy warm.

STORAGE

The cookies can be stored in an airtight container at room temperature for up to 1 week or in the refrigerator for up to 2 weeks. They also freeze well and can be frozen for up to 2 months.

RASPBERRY PARTY POPS

Part no-bake cheesecake and part white chocolate rocky road, these party pops are probably the most luscious dessert you can eat on a stick. The hundreds and thousands and raspberries are Aussie favourites and make them look irresistibly fun. And they are so simple to whip together to serve at parties. Your friends will think you're a party-pop-pushing genius!

MAKES 16

500 g (1 lb 2 oz) cream cheese, softened
200 g (7 oz) good-quality white chocolate, chopped
5 pink marshmallows, chopped
6 gummy raspberries, chopped
16 ice cream sticks

1. Using an electric mixer fitted with the paddle attachment, beat the cream cheese until smooth.

2. Melt the chocolate using either the microwave or double-boiler method (see page 245). Add to the cream cheese and beat until combined. Fold in the chopped marshmallows and gummy raspberries.

3. Spoon the mixture into 16 mini silicone popsicle moulds, about 4 x 7 cm (1½ x 2¾ inches) each. Gently tap on the bench to remove air pockets. Insert an ice cream stick into each mould and smooth the top. Place in the freezer for at least 1 hour or until very firm.

ASSEMBLY AND DECORATION

400 g (14 oz) good-quality white chocolate, chopped
2½ tablespoons coconut oil
20 gummy raspberries, halved (optional)
Hundreds and thousands or rainbow sprinkles (optional)

1. Melt the chocolate and coconut oil using either the microwave or double-boiler method. Stir until combined. Transfer into a deep jug or glass for ease of dipping. Allow to cool slightly.

2. Working with one at a time, gently unmould the party pops and dip them into the melted chocolate until covered. Gently shake off the excess, place on a sheet of baking paper and quickly decorate with the sliced gummy raspberries and sprinkles, if using. Wait until the chocolate has set before serving or storing.

STORAGE

The party pops are best served immediately after decorating or eaten straight from the fridge. They can be refrigerated in an airtight container for up to 2 weeks, or frozen for up to 2 months.

FLAMIN' GALAH CUPCAKES

A flamin' galah: Australian slang for someone who is a bit daft, but loveable nonetheless. The friendly galah is my absolute favourite bird of the cockatoo family: not only do pink and grey work fabulously well together as a colour combination, but galahs can often be found showing off and larking around with their mates. These scrumptious cupcakes are filled with character, and make the perfect easy treat for your own loveable little clowns.

MAKES 12

VANILLA CUPCAKES

⅓ cup (80 g) unsalted butter, softened
½ cup (110 g) caster sugar
1 teaspoon vanilla bean paste or vanilla extract
2 eggs, at room temperature
1 pinch salt
1 cup (160 g) self-raising flour
⅔ cup (160 ml) milk, at room temperature

1. Preheat the oven to 160°C (320°F) fan forced. Line a 12-hole cupcake tray with cupcake cases.
2. Using an electric mixer, cream the butter, sugar and vanilla until light and fluffy. Add the eggs, one at a time, beating until combined. Add the salt.
3. Alternately fold in the flour and the milk, in one-third increments. Fold until just combined.
4. Divide the batter evenly among the cupcake cases, filling each one about three-quarters full.
5. Bake for 20 minutes or until a toothpick inserted into the centre of one of the cupcakes comes out clean. Remove from the oven and transfer to a wire rack to cool completely.

VANILLA BUTTERCREAM

50 g (1¾ oz) unsalted butter, softened
1½ cups (210 g) icing (confectioners') sugar, sifted
1½ tablespoons milk
½ teaspoon vanilla bean paste or vanilla extract
Black and pink food colouring

1. Using an electric mixer, beat the butter until very pale. Gradually add the icing sugar while beating on low speed. Add the milk and vanilla and beat on high speed until fluffy.
2. Divide the buttercream into two bowls. Colour one bowl grey by mixing in a small amount of black food colouring, and colour the second bowl pink by mixing in a small amount of pink food colouring.

ASSEMBLY AND DECORATION

12 white marshmallows
12 brown Smarties
Black food paint or black food dye
12 pink marshmallows
24 cashew nuts

1. Use a butter knife or small offset spatula to apply grey buttercream in feather-like strokes to the top half of each cupcake. Repeat the same technique on the bottom halves using pink buttercream.

2. Place a white marshmallow in the centre of each cupcake. Paint the Smarties black using the food paint or food dye. Use a small amount of buttercream to stick the painted Smarties onto the marshmallows.

3. Use a pair of clean, sharp scissors to cut each pink marshmallow horizontally into three slices. Place above the marshmallow eye to create the crest of each galah.

4. Use the cashew nuts to create a beak for each galah cupcake. Now they're ready to squawk!

Decorating Tip

- If you're avoiding nuts, you could use jellybeans instead of cashews for the galahs' beaks.

WATERMELON JELLY

Wibble wobble, wibble wobble, jelly on a plate. I adore jelly – and this kitsch version brings a little extra creative flair to a simple dessert. I'm yet to meet an Aussie who doesn't remember watermelon slices as a thirst-quenching summer snack and, like many of my mates, I find the watermelon motif VERY aesthetically pleasing: a blissfully summery reminder of childhood.

SERVES 8

2 x 85 g (3 oz) packets strawberry jelly (although 10 points if you can find watermelon!)

¼ cup (50 g) dark chocolate chips

85 g (3 oz) packet 'Create a Jelly' (see tip)

2½ tablespoons full-cream milk, at room temperature

Green food colouring

STORAGE

This easy recipe can be made up to 4 days ahead. Just cover the top of the jelly bowl with plastic wrap or a beeswax wrap and unmould it when you're ready to serve.

1. In a heatproof jug, prepare the strawberry jelly according to the packet instructions. Set aside at room temperature until lukewarm.

2. Pour the strawberry jelly mixture into a 20 cm (8 inch) round cake tin. Refrigerate for 30 minutes or until slightly firm.

3. Place the chocolate chips around the top of the jelly layer. Return to the refrigerator for another 30 minutes.

4. Prepare the 'Create a Jelly' mixture according to the packet instructions. Combine one-third of the mixture with the milk and gently pour on top of the strawberry jelly. Refrigerate for 30 minutes or until slightly firm.

5. Combine the remaining 'Create a Jelly' mixture with 1–2 drops of green food colouring. Gently pour the mixture on top of the milk jelly and refrigerate for at least 4 hours or until completely set.

6. To serve the jelly, place the cake tin in a sink filled with hot water for about 5–10 seconds. (Alternatively, half-fill a larger bowl with hot water and sit the cake tin in the water for about 5–10 seconds – the bowl needs to be large enough to fit the cake tin, but be careful not to let any water overflow into the jelly.) Carefully turn out onto a serving plate. The jelly is best enjoyed chilled, sliced into wedges. It's lovely served with vanilla ice cream.

Decorating Tip

- If you can't find 'Create a Jelly', simply dissolve 3 teaspoons powdered gelatine, ½ cup (110 g) caster sugar and ½ teaspoon vanilla extract in 1½ cups (375 ml) hot water.

OPAL COOKIES

Well, aren't these dazzlers? The opal is considered the national gemstone of Australia, with our precious treasure trove of a country apparently accounting for over 90 per cent of the world's supply. The background colour of opals can be white, black (most rare), or almost any colour of the visual spectrum, so these cookies are limited only by your own creativity! Edible glitter is used here to capture the opal's stunning iridescence — you can find it in a variety of colours in most cake decorating stores. And opal is the birthstone for October, but don't let that hold you back: I give these as a gift all year round.

MAKES 12

SUGAR COOKIES

1½ cups (240 g) plain flour, sifted
½ teaspoon salt
100 g (3½ oz) unsalted butter, softened
½ cup (110 g) caster sugar
1 egg, chilled
1 teaspoon vanilla extract or vanilla bean paste

1. Sift the flour and salt into a large bowl.
2. Using an electric mixer fitted with the paddle attachment, cream the butter and sugar until fluffy and pale. Beat in the egg.
3. Add the flour mixture and mix on low speed until thoroughly combined. Mix in the vanilla.
4. Form the dough into a ball and place on a large piece of plastic wrap. Wrap the sides of the plastic over the ball, then press down with the palm of your hand to make a disc about 2.5 cm (1 inch) thick. Finish wrapping the disc with the plastic. Chill the dough for about 30 minutes.
5. Unwrap the dough, place on a large piece of baking paper or silicone mat and roll out until 5 mm (¼ inch) thick. Slide the baking paper or mat and dough onto a board, then refrigerate for about 15 minutes.
6. Preheat the oven to 160°C (320°F) fan forced. Line two baking trays with baking paper or silicone baking mats.
7. Cut the chilled dough into shapes using an 8 cm (3¼ inch) round or oval cookie cutter. Place on the lined trays, leaving 2.5 cm (1 inch) clearance around each one. Reserve any excess dough.
8. Put the trays of cookies in the freezer for 15 minutes. Transfer the trays to the oven and bake the cookies for 12–15 minutes or until the edges are slightly golden. Leave the trays on wire racks to cool for 15 minutes, then gently remove the cookies to finish cooling.
9. Repeat the rolling, cutting and baking with the remaining cookie dough.

ASSEMBLY AND DECORATION

Cornflour, for rolling
200 g (7 oz) white fondant
Edible sugar glue (see tips)
Edible glitter in different colours
   and varieties

1. On a surface lightly dusted with cornflour, roll out the fondant to about 2 mm (1/16 inch) thick. Use cookie cutters to cut enough fondant rounds or ovals to cover all of the cookies.

2. Apply a very small amount of sugar glue onto each fondant shape and stick it onto a cookie.

3. Apply a very small amount of sugar glue onto the fondant and decorate with the various types of edible glitter to create an opal effect. Leave to dry for at least 2 hours before packaging.

STORAGE

- Once the decorated cookies have dried, store them in an airtight container at room temperature for up to 2 weeks.
- The undecorated cookies can be stored for up to 2 weeks in an airtight container. They also freeze well.

Decorating Tips

- Use 100 g (3½ oz) white fondant and 100 g (3½ oz) black fondant to create different types of opals.
- Edible glitter can be found in cake decorating stores and online.
- You can use water and a clean brush instead of edible sugar glue.

KOALA CRUNCH POPS

You'll find your friends clinging to these little cuties just as tightly as a koala clings to a gum tree. The crunching and munching will be joyful, and you can make believe you're in a eucalypt forest filled with cuddly marsupials absentmindedly chewing their bodyweight in gum leaves. Puffed rice cereal gives these pops their crunch and variations on the recipe are easy – try a white choc version, or add peanut butter to the mix, and freeze-dried fruit pieces for a pop of extra flavour.

MAKES 16

300 g (10½ oz) good-quality dark
 chocolate, chopped
2½ tablespoons coconut oil
2 cups (80 g) puffed rice cereal
½ cup (45 g) desiccated coconut
16 ice cream sticks

1. Melt the chocolate and coconut oil using either the microwave or double-boiler method (see page 245). Stir until combined. Remove from the heat and mix in the puffed rice and coconut.

2. Spoon the filling into 16 mini silicone popsicle moulds, about 4 x 7 cm (1½ x 2¾ inches) each. Gently tap on the bench to remove air pockets. Insert an ice cream stick into each mould and use the back of a spoon to further compact the filling into the mould. Place in the freezer for at least 30 minutes or until very firm.

ASSEMBLY AND DECORATION

500 g (1 lb 2 oz) good-quality white
 chocolate, chopped
2 tablespoons coconut oil
Black oil-based or powdered
 chocolate colouring
32 white chocolate melts
32 natural almonds
32 sugar flower decorations
8 gummy spearmint leaves, halved
Black food colouring pen or black
 food paint

1. Melt the white chocolate and coconut oil using either the microwave or double-boiler method. Tint with black chocolate colouring until a grey colour is achieved. Transfer into a deep jug or glass for ease of dipping.

2. Unmould the crunch pops. Use the melted chocolate to attach two white chocolate melts to the top of each crunch pop to make ears, and also add an almond 'nose' and 'arm'.

3. One by one, dip the crunch pops into the melted chocolate until covered. Gently tap off the excess chocolate and place on a sheet of baking paper. Before the chocolate hardens, decorate the ears with sugar flowers and attach the spearmint gummy halves just below the nose. Allow to set completely at room temperature (at least 1 hour).

4. Once the chocolate has completely set, use a black food pen or black food paint and a thin brush to draw each koala's eyes. Next, colour in the nose and draw in a tiny smile, as well as some claws.

Decorating Tips

- I used Cadbury White Chocolate Melts for the ears.
- You can buy sugar flowers from supermarkets or cake decorating stores. You could also use pink marshmallows, cut to size.
- I used Edible Art Paint and a thin brush to add the final details to the koalas.
- To make nut-free crunch pops, replace the natural almonds with jellybeans that have been cut in half lengthways.

STORAGE

Store the crunch pops in an airtight container. They will keep at room temperature for 1 week or in the fridge for 2 weeks, and can be frozen for 2 months. Serve straight from the refrigerator or at room temperature.

BEDAZZLED ICE CREAM SAMBOS

Aussies are funny about long words: who can be bothered to say afternoon, when arvo will do? Or avocado, when we all know the best fruit in the world is the avo? Even the name of our fair nation gets shortened to Straya. So, when the rellies come for a barbie, serve them up an ice cream sambo. Bake the cookies in advance and have ice cream and plenty of toppings ready to go — freeze-dried fruit pieces, crushed nuts or pretzels, mini chocolate chips and toasted coconut.

MAKES 10

CHOCOLATE-STUDDED COOKIES

¾ cup (180 g) unsalted butter, softened
¾ cup (165 g) caster sugar
½ cup (80 g) dark brown sugar
1 teaspoon vanilla bean paste
1 egg, chilled
2½ cups (400 g) plain flour
½ teaspoon salt
1 cup (170 g) candy-coated chocolates

1. Preheat the oven to 160°C (320°F) fan forced. Line two baking trays with baking paper.
2. Using an electric mixer fitted with the paddle attachment, beat the butter, caster sugar and brown sugar for 5 minutes or until light and fluffy.
3. Add the vanilla and egg and beat until well combined. Add the flour and salt and beat until just combined. Refrigerate the cookie dough for at least 30 minutes so that it firms up and is easier to handle.
4. Roll the dough into balls the size of a golf ball and place on the trays, leaving 5 cm (2 inches) clearance around each one. Gently flatten each cookie and stud with the candy-coated chocolates.
5. Working in batches, bake the cookies for 20 minutes or just until golden. Cool on a wire rack.

ASSEMBLY AND DECORATION

4 cups (1 litre) ice cream
2 cups (70 g) Froot Loops, crushed
½ cup (90 g) rainbow sprinkles

1. Working quickly, place a big scoop of ice cream onto a cookie and gently press another cookie on top. Repeat with the remaining cookies.
2. Press the crushed Froot Loops or sprinkles onto the sides of the sambos (or roll the sambos in the Froot Loops and sprinkles) and tuck in!

STORAGE

The ice cream sambos are best enjoyed immediately or frozen for up to 3 days.

Decorating Tip

- I used chocolate, rainbow and vanilla ice cream, but you can use whatever flavour you like.

FANCY FLIP-FLOP COOKIES

These were apparently made fashionable by the ancient Egyptians. Tell 'em they're dreaming: Aussies have been attached to their loyal thongs since the beginning of time. In fact, we love these rubbery foot mats so much that we've shuffled them off our sandy beaches and all the way into city life, flip-flopping around shopping malls and into business meetings (it was a Friday and I have no regrets). The cookie version is always just as welcome... Take these anywhere and watch people's faces light up, as if they're greeting an old friend.

MAKES 10

SUGAR COOKIES

1½ cups (240 g) plain flour, sifted
½ teaspoon salt
100 g (3½ oz) unsalted butter, softened
½ cup (110 g) caster sugar
1 egg, chilled
1 teaspoon vanilla extract or vanilla bean paste

1. Sift the flour and salt into a large bowl.

2. Using an electric mixer fitted with the paddle attachment, cream the butter and sugar until fluffy and pale. Beat in the egg.

3. Add the flour mixture and mix on low speed until thoroughly combined. Mix in the vanilla.

4. Form the dough into a ball and place on a large piece of plastic wrap. Wrap the sides of the plastic over the ball, then press down with the palm of your hand to make a disc about 2.5 cm (1 inch) thick. Finish wrapping the disc with the plastic. Chill the dough for about 30 minutes.

5. Unwrap the dough, place on a large piece of baking paper or silicone mat and roll out until 5 mm (¼ inch) thick. Slide the baking paper or mat and dough onto a board, then refrigerate for about 15 minutes.

6. Preheat the oven to 160°C (320°F) fan forced. Line two baking trays with baking paper or silicone baking mats.

7. Use a cookie cutter or a small, sharp knife to cut the chilled dough into flip-flop shapes. Place on the lined trays, leaving 2.5 cm (1 inch) clearance around each one. Reserve any excess dough.

8. Put the trays of cookies in the freezer for 15 minutes. Transfer the trays to the oven and bake the cookies for 12–15 minutes or until the edges are slightly golden. Leave the trays on wire racks to cool for 15 minutes, then gently remove the cookies to finish cooling.

9. Repeat the rolling, cutting and baking with the remaining cookie dough.

ASSEMBLY AND DECORATION

10 rainbow fruit Roll-Ups
50 g (1¾ oz) white chocolate, chopped
50 g (1¾ oz) dark chocolate, chopped
Black liquorice rope
Assorted sugar decorations

1. Unroll and flatten the fruit Roll-Ups. Using a cookie cutter or sharp kitchen scissors, cut the fruit Roll-ups to fit the cookies.

2. Melt the white chocolate using either the microwave or double-boiler method (see page 245). Use the melted chocolate to stick the fruit Roll-Ups shapes onto the cookies.

3. Melt the dark chocolate using either the microwave or double-boiler method.

4. Slice the liquorice to make two straps for each flip-flop cookie, about 5 cm (2 inches) long. Use a small amount of the melted dark chocolate to stick them in place.

5. Use the melted dark chocolate to stick the sugar decorations onto the flip-flop straps.

STORAGE

- Once the decorated cookies have dried, store them in an airtight container at room temperature for up to 2 weeks.
- The undecorated cookies can be stored for up to 2 weeks in an airtight container. They also freeze well.

Decorating Tips

- I used a 10 x 6 cm (4 x 2½ inch) cookie cutter. You can use the cookie cutter to mark an impression in the fruit Roll-Ups to guide your cutting.
- I found the mini flowers, emojis and rainbows in the baking aisle of my local supermarket.

GOLD RUSH HONEYCOMB

Eureka! You've discovered a treasure of a recipe. When gold nuggets were found in Victoria in the 1850s, the rush was on to get there and get digging. Step away from the plate: you'll have the same rush when you give the gift of edible gold. Making your own honeycomb requires a bit of care and attention, but the dazzlingly delicious results are well worth it. Pack these beauties into gift boxes or airtight bags and create your own boom time, or use them to decorate cupcakes or cakes.

MAKES ABOUT 30 PIECES

Cooking oil spray
250 g (9 oz) golden syrup or liquid glucose
250 g (9 oz) caster sugar
3 teaspoons bicarbonate of soda (baking soda)

1. Grease a foil-lined cake tin with cooking oil spray.
2. Combine the golden syrup and sugar in a large saucepan. Stir over medium heat just until the sugar dissolves. Bring to the boil and cook, without stirring, until the mixture reaches hard-crack stage – 150°C (300°F) on a candy thermometer.
3. Remove the pan from the heat. Carefully whisk in the bicarbonate of soda (the hot sugar mixture will bubble and sputter and increase in volume).
4. Carefully pour the mixture into the cake tin. Set aside to cool, without disturbing, for at least 2 hours. Once cooled, break the honeycomb into pieces.

DECORATION

400 g (14 oz) good-quality dark chocolate, chopped
1¼ tablespoons coconut oil
Edible gold powder (optional)

1. Melt the chocolate and coconut oil using either the microwave or double-boiler method (see page 245). Stir until combined.
2. Dip the honeycomb pieces into the melted chocolate and place on a sheet of baking paper to set at room temperature.
3. Once the chocolate has set, use a clean dusting brush to cover the honeycomb pieces with edible gold powder, if using.

STORAGE

Store the honeycomb in an airtight container between sheets of waxed paper for up to a week.

Decorating Tips

- I love using bitter dark chocolate to coat the honeycomb.
- I used a 33 x 23 cm (13 x 9 inch) cake tin.

FRUIT TINGLES® CAKE

Fruit Tingles aren't the feeling you get when a pineapple strokes the back of your neck. These chalky characters are a favourite brand of confectionery – delightfully multicoloured, disc-shaped, fruit-flavoured lollies that originated proudly in Australia. When I was a little girl, I especially loved their tart sherbet flavour, which leaves a gentle fruity fizziness in your mouth. I have a theory that Champagne is the adult version of Fruit Tingles, distilled into liquid form for easier ingestion. This cake is another exciting variation on the theme. The buttercream is everything you'd expect it to be and, sandwiched between layers of fluffy sponge cake, the humble lolly is raised to spine-tingling heights.

SERVES 12

VANILLA SPONGE CAKE

⅔ cup (160 g) unsalted butter, softened
1 cup (220 g) caster sugar
1½ cups (240 g) self-raising flour, sifted
1 teaspoon vanilla extract
4 eggs, lightly whisked
2 tablespoons hot water

1. Preheat the oven to 160°C (320°F) fan forced. Lightly grease two 18 cm (7 inch) round cake tins and line the base of each tin with baking paper.

2. Using an electric mixer, beat the butter and sugar until light, pale and creamy. Add 2 tablespoons of the flour, then gradually add the vanilla and eggs, beating well after each addition.

3. Gently fold in the remaining flour and the hot water.

4. Divide the mixture equally between the cake tins. Bake for 20–25 minutes or until the centre of each cake springs back when lightly pressed. Leave in the tins for 5 minutes before transferring to a wire rack to cool completely. Cover and set aside until needed.

FRUIT TINGLES BUTTERCREAM

2 cups (500 g) salted butter, softened
2 cups (280 g) icing (confectioners') sugar, sifted
1 teaspoon vanilla bean paste
2 x 34 g (1 oz) rolls Fruit Tingles, finely crushed (see tips)
½ cup (90 g) rainbow sprinkles (see tips)

1. Using an electric mixer, beat the butter on high speed for 10–15 minutes or until doubled in size and very pale.

2. Add the icing sugar, in one-third increments, and beat until incorporated and fluffy.

3. Beat in the vanilla, then beat in the crushed Fruit Tingles and sprinkles until evenly distributed.

ASSEMBLY AND DECORATION

3 x 34 g (1 oz) rolls Fruit Tingles

1. Roughly crush two-thirds of the Fruit Tingles. Set aside.

2. Working on a cake turntable or lazy Susan, secure the bottom layer of cake onto a cake plate or board with a dollop of buttercream and then gently twist in place. Use an offset spatula to cover the top of the cake with a layer of buttercream, about 1 cm (½ inch) thick, spreading it right to the edge.

3. Place the second layer of cake on top and gently press down to secure. Using an offset spatula and a cake scraper, gently crumb coat the entire cake with a thin layer of buttercream (see page 240). Carefully smooth the side until the desired finish is achieved. Chill in the refrigerator for 10–15 minutes.

4. Apply another layer of buttercream to the chilled cake and use the cake scraper and offset spatula to smooth the side and top (see page 241) – or you may choose a more rustic finish.

5. Using the picture as a guide, decorate the top and side of the cake with the crushed and whole Fruit Tingles.

Decorating Tips

- The lighter in colour the butter that you use for the buttercream is, the better.
- The easiest way to crush the Fruit Tingles is by using a food processor. You can also put them in a resealable plastic bag and smash them with a rolling pin. They need to be crushed until very fine – almost like dust.
- I used rainbow jimmies in the buttercream as they don't 'bleed' and lose their colour the way regular hundreds and thousands do.
- When making buttercream, I turn off the mixer to add the icing sugar and then slowly turn it back up to full speed to incorporate it.

STORAGE

The cake can be refrigerated for up to 3 days. It is best served at room temperature.

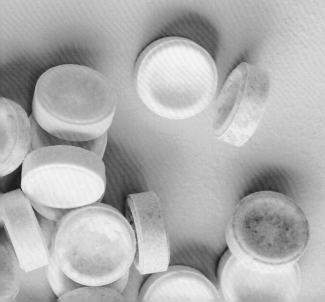

REDBACK SPIDER CUPCAKES

Our great southern land is home to one of the world's most notoriously dangerous spiders, the redback. It's an infamous Aussie icon (along with sharks, snakes, crocodiles and Pauline Hanson) that's highly venomous and instantly recognisable. These cupcakes can be made as any kind of spider, but Mother Nature has told us time and time again that black and red go so well together. I read that when a redback first confronts its prey it doesn't bite, so enjoy the element of surprise and dig in first!

MAKES 12

CHOCOLATE CUPCAKES

⅓ cup (80 g) unsalted butter,
  softened
½ cup (110 g) caster sugar
1 teaspoon vanilla extract
2 eggs, at room temperature
1 pinch salt
1 cup (160 g) self-raising flour
⅓ cup (35 g) cocoa powder
¾ cup (185 ml) milk, at room
  temperature

1. Preheat the oven to 160°C (320°F) fan forced. Line a 12-hole cupcake tray with cupcake cases.
2. Using an electric mixer, cream the butter, sugar and vanilla until light and fluffy. Add the eggs, one at a time, beating until combined. Add the salt.
3. Alternately fold in the flour, cocoa and milk, in one-third increments. Fold until just combined.
4. Divide the batter evenly among the cupcake cases, filling each one about three-quarters full.
5. Bake for 20 minutes or until a toothpick inserted into the centre of one of the cupcakes comes out clean. Remove from the oven and transfer to a wire rack to cool completely.

VANILLA BUTTERCREAM

50 g (1¾ oz) unsalted butter,
  softened
1½ cups (210 g) icing (confectioners')
  sugar, sifted
1½ tablespoons milk
1 teaspoon vanilla bean paste or
  vanilla extract
Red food colouring

1. Using an electric mixer, beat the butter until very pale. Gradually add the icing sugar while beating on low speed. Add the milk and vanilla and beat on high speed until fluffy.
2. Colour the buttercream by mixing in red food colouring until the desired shade is achieved.

ASSEMBLY AND DECORATION

2 strawberry fruit Roll-Ups
12 large chocolate balls
12 small chocolate balls
Black liquorice rope

1. Use a butter knife or small offset spatula to apply a generous dollop of buttercream to each cupcake.

2. Use a sharp knife or kitchen scissors to cut the fruit Roll-Ups into strips. Wrap a strip around each of the large round chocolates and place each one on the top of a cupcake to make the spiders' abdomens.

3. Slice or cut small triangles of the fruit Roll-Ups to make eyes. Stick the eyes onto the smaller round chocolates to make the spiders' heads, using a little buttercream as glue, if needed. Place a head next to the abdomen on each cupcake.

4. To make the spiders' legs, slice or cut thin strips from the liquorice, about 4 cm (1½ inches) long. Arrange four strips on the side of each abdomen.

Decorating Tips

- If you colour the buttercream at least 24 hours ahead, you'll achieve a richer red colour. Cover and refrigerate the buttercream, then bring it back to room temperature and beat until fluffy.
- I used dark chocolate Lindt Lindor Balls for the spiders' abdomens and Dark Maltesers for their heads.
- You can use any kind of red-coloured fruit straps to add the details to the spiders.

STORAGE

The cupcakes are best eaten on the day of decorating, but they can be refrigerated in an airtight container for up to 3 days.

TOASTY ANZAC SLICE

I firmly believe the best Anzac biscuits are always home-made. It's the only way to achieve those gloriously buttery and chewy qualities we all love. The comforting combination of vanilla marshmallow, bitter dark chocolate and toasted coconut flakes makes this a slice that is worthy of our local legends. We thank you for what you have sacrificed for our country.

MAKES 18 BARS

BISCUIT BASE

2 cups (200 g) rolled oats
1 cup (160 g) self-raising flour, sifted
½ cup (110 g) caster sugar
½ cup (40 g) shredded coconut
⅓ cup (120 g) golden syrup, warmed
½ cup (125 g) unsalted butter, melted
1 pinch salt

MARSHMALLOW FILLING

250 g (9 oz) caster sugar
½ cup (125 ml) water
2 large egg whites
70 ml (2¼ fl oz) warm water
1½ tablespoons powdered gelatine
1 teaspoon vanilla bean paste

TOPPING

200 g (7 oz) good-quality dark chocolate, chopped
1¼ tablespoons coconut oil
1½ cups (75 g) toasted coconut flakes

STORAGE

Store the slice in an airtight container for 3 days. You can also refrigerate it for 1 week or freeze it for up to 2 months.

1. Preheat the oven to 160°C (320°F) fan forced. Line a 25.5 cm (10 inch) square cake tin with baking paper. Allow the baking paper to extend over two sides to make it easier to remove the slice from the tin.

2. To make the biscuit base, combine all of the ingredients in a bowl and mix well. Press into the cake tin. Bake for 20 minutes or until light golden. Allow to cool before topping with the marshmallow layer.

3. To make the filling, place the sugar and ½ cup of water in a large heavy-based saucepan. Bring to the boil over high heat, without stirring. Once the sugar syrup reaches 110°C (230°F) on a candy thermometer, use an electric mixer to whip the egg whites into firm peaks. Continue cooking the syrup.

4. Meanwhile, pour the warm water into a small bowl and add the gelatine.

5. When the syrup reaches 120°C (250°F), remove the pan from the heat and gently stir in the gelatine mixture until well combined. With the mixer on the highest speed, continue to whip the egg whites whilst carefully pouring in the hot syrup. Whip until the mixture thickens and increases in volume, but remains pourable. Mix in the vanilla.

6. Working quickly, pour the filling over the base. Use an offset spatula to smooth the surface, if needed. Refrigerate for at least 1 hour or until completely set.

7. To make the topping, melt the chocolate and coconut oil using either the microwave or double-boiler method (see page 245). Stir until combined.

8. Spread the topping over the filling and immediately sprinkle with the toasted coconut flakes. Refrigerate until set.

9. Remove the slice from the tin. Using a sharp knife dipped in hot water, cut into bars to serve.

BUDGIE SMUGGLERS

You can spot them at a beach near you, or you can 'sun bake' in them from the safety of your own kitchen. We even had a Prime Minister who enjoyed running around in his budgie smugglers. I like to encourage diversity and creativity when it comes to whipping up this cheeky homage to our iconic, super-snug-fitting Australian men's beachwear. I think I've said enough... GO NUTS!

MAKES 12

LEMON CUPCAKES

⅓ cup (80 g) unsalted butter, softened
½ cup (110 g) caster sugar
1 teaspoon vanilla bean paste or vanilla extract
1 tablespoon grated lemon zest
2 eggs, at room temperature
1 pinch salt
1 cup (160 g) self-raising flour
⅔ cup (160 ml) milk, at room temperature
2 tablespoons lemon juice

1. Preheat the oven to 160°C (320°F) fan forced. Line a 12-hole cupcake tray with cupcake cases.

2. Using an electric mixer, cream the butter, sugar, vanilla and lemon zest until light and fluffy. Add the eggs, one at a time, beating until combined. Add the salt.

3. Alternately fold in the flour and the milk, in one-third increments. Add the lemon juice and fold until just combined.

4. Divide the batter evenly among the cupcake cases, filling each one about three-quarters full.

5. Bake for 20 minutes or until a toothpick inserted into the centre of one of the cupcakes comes out clean. Remove from the oven and transfer to a wire rack to cool completely.

VANILLA BUTTERCREAM

50 g (1¾ oz) unsalted butter, softened
1½ cups (210 g) icing (confectioners') sugar, sifted
1½ tablespoons milk
1 teaspoon vanilla extract
Orange food colouring
2 tablespoons cocoa powder

1. Using an electric mixer, beat the butter until very pale. Gradually add the icing sugar while beating on low speed. Add the milk and vanilla and beat on high speed until fluffy.

2. Divide the buttercream into three bowls. Colour one bowl peach by mixing in a small amount of orange food colouring, and the second bowl brown by mixing in the cocoa. Leave the last bowl white.

ASSEMBLY AND DECORATION

12 cashew nuts
4 rainbow fruit Roll-Ups
2 teaspoons chocolate sprinkles
2 teaspoons orange sprinkles
2 teaspoons desiccated coconut

1. Use a butter knife or small offset spatula to cover a third of the cupcakes with peach buttercream, a third of the cupcakes with brown buttercream and a third of the cupcakes with white buttercream.

2. Place a cashew nut on the bottom half of each cupcake.

3. Use a scalpel or sharp scissors to cut out swimming briefs from the fruit Roll-Ups. You'll need 12 in total. Make sure each pair is large enough to cover the cashew... actually, I'll leave that up to you! Arrange a pair of swimming briefs on top of each cupcake, over the cashew, and gently press in place to secure.

4. Decorate the cupcakes with the sprinkles or coconut for a 'hairy' effect (if that's your thing).

Decorating Tip

- If you're avoiding nuts, use jellybeans or mini jellybeans instead of the cashews.

STORAGE

These cupcakes are best eaten on the day they're decorated, but they can be refrigerated in an airtight container for up to 3 days.

GOONBAG JELLY

Cheap boxed wine ('chateau cardboard') is a 1965 Aussie invention and cultural icon (yep — see our chests swell with patriotic pride). The wine inside the box is in a silver space bag, which can be inflated into a handy pillow to rest your head on when you've drunk the 'goon'. You might have enjoyed a Goon Sunrise (our cost-effective Aussie alternative to the Tequila Sunrise), but have you tried the slightly fancier Goonbag Jelly? It's easy on the eye, and easy on the palate... just like an edible sunrise.

SERVES 12

Cooking oil spray

2 x 85 g (3 oz) packets orange jelly

400 ml (14 fl oz) of your favourite white wine (no judgement if it pours from a silver pillow!)

800 g (1 lb 12 oz) tin peaches, drained and cut into chunks

2 x 85 g (3 oz) packets strawberry jelly

STORAGE

This recipe can be made up to 5 days ahead. Just cover the top of the jelly bowl with plastic wrap or a beeswax wrap and unmould it when you're ready to serve.

1. Grease a large jelly mould or bowl with cooking oil spray.

2. In a heatproof jug, prepare the 2 packets of orange jelly according to the packet instructions, replacing 300 ml (10½ fl oz) of the cold water with 200 ml (7 fl oz) white wine. Stir in the remaining 100 ml (3½ fl oz) cold water. Pour into the jelly mould or bowl and add half of the chopped peaches. Refrigerate for 2 hours or until slightly firm.

3. Prepare the 2 packets of strawberry jelly in the same way as the orange jelly, replacing 300 ml (10½ fl oz) of the cold water with 200 ml (7 fl oz) white wine and stirring in the remaining 100 ml (3½ fl oz) cold water. Allow to cool to room temperature. Gently pour on top of the orange jelly and add the remaining chopped peaches. Refrigerate until completely set (at least 4 hours).

4. To serve the jelly, place the jelly bowl in a sink filled with hot water for about 5–10 seconds. (Alternatively, half-fill a larger bowl with hot water and sit the jelly bowl in the water for about 5–10 seconds — the bowl needs to be large enough to fit the jelly bowl, but be careful not to let any water overflow into the jelly.) Carefully turn the jelly out onto a serving plate and... ta-da! The jelly is best enjoyed chilled, sliced into wedges. If you're feeling fancy, serve it with vanilla ice cream for an extra-delicious treat.

CHAPTER 2

SHE'LL BE RIGHT

Congratulations: you've mastered the easy stuff, so what now?
Shoot for the stars and make a Byron Bay Kombi Van cake,
that's what! There's still nothing tricky, and every recipe is broken
down into easy steps – so you'll be right!

EDIBLE OUTBACK TERRARIUM

Nothing says Australia quite like the Outback. This vast and remote area of inland Australia epitomises not only our pioneering identity, but also our entirely unique array of creepies and crawlies, slitheries and scalies! That red earth might look parched and empty at first glance, but get down and take a closer look and you'll discover beetles, bugs, lizards, spiders, scorpions and ants — many of them found only on our great island continent. Dig down into the delicious layers of this edible terrarium and become one with the great outdoors.

SERVES 12

CHOCOLATE FILLING

500 g (1 lb 2 oz) cream cheese, softened
50 g (1¾ oz) unsalted butter, softened
1 cup (250 ml) single (pure) cream
½ cup (55 g) cocoa powder
½ cup (70 g) icing (confectioners') sugar, sifted

1. Using an electric mixer, beat the cream cheese and butter until fluffy. With the motor running, gradually add the cream.
2. Add the cocoa and icing sugar and beat until combined.
3. Cover and refrigerate until you're ready to assemble the terrarium.

LOLLY INSECTS

Assorted lollies, such as sour worms, gummy snakes, banana lollies, jellybeans, milk bottles, gummy spearmint leaves, strawberries and cream lollies, peaches and cream lollies, liquorice allsorts, Smarties, rainbow sour straps, ladybird sugar decorations
4 flaked almonds
1 green Pocky stick
Black liquorice rope
Blue and yellow writing icing

1. Make the lolly insects, using the examples shown on page 69 as a guide. Use a small, sharp knife to slice the lollies and a pair of kitchen scissors to cut the liquorice rope. Use the writing icing to add details to the wings.

ASSEMBLY AND DECORATION

¼ cup (25 g) desiccated coconut

Green food colouring

200 g (7 oz) Anzac biscuits or
  digestive biscuits, crushed

1 glass terrarium bowl

1 x 15 cm (6 inch) chocolate cake
  (store-bought or home-made)

⅓ cup (65 g) dark chocolate chips

¼ cup (50 g) Reese's peanut butter
  chips

50 g (1¾ oz) chocolate rocks

50 g (1¾ oz) chocolate cookies,
  crushed

STORAGE

The chocolate filling can be
made several days in advance
and refrigerated until needed.
Most of the lolly insects can
also be prepared ahead and
stored in an airtight container.
I recommend assembling the
terrarium on the day you are
serving it, so the layers don't
get too soggy.

1. Put the coconut in a resealable plastic bag and add a few drops of green colouring. Seal the bag, then shake the bag and massage the coconut until it reaches the desired shade.

2. Spread the crushed Anzac biscuits over the base of a glass terrarium bowl, reserving a few tablespoons for decorating. Add the chocolate cake, cutting it to fit, then add the chocolate filling and smooth the surface.

3. Decorate the top of the terrarium with the chocolate chips, peanut butter chips, chocolate rocks, coloured coconut, remaining crushed Anzac biscuits and crushed chocolate cookies. Arrange an assortment of creepy, crawly lolly insects on top.

Decorating Tips

- If you don't have a glass terrarium bowl, look around your kitchen to see what else you could use, such as a rectangular glass baking dish.
- I used lollies that I found in the confectionery aisle of my local supermarket, but you may come across some even better options and creative ideas!
- For a nut-free cake, replace the peanut butter chips with white chocolate chips and omit the flaked almonds when making the lolly insects.

CHOC FRECKLE POPS CAKE

I reckon I've popped far too many chocolate freckles in my life! I had no idea they were so super-easy to make – although perhaps I'm not to be trusted with a whole bag of hundreds and thousands? When you make these yourself, you can use your favourite chocolate (milk, dark or white) AND your favourite sprinkles. Bring lollipop sticks into the picture, and you've got a whole new party treat. Stick them in the top of a cake or serve them as they are – perfect for party-goers who don't want sticky fingers.

SERVES 20

CHOC-HEAVEN CAKE

Cooking oil spray
2 cups (320 g) self-raising flour
1¾ cups (385 g) caster sugar
¾ cup (85 g) cocoa powder
½ teaspoon bicarbonate of soda
   (baking soda)
½ teaspoon salt
1 teaspoon instant coffee powder
   (optional)
1 cup (250 ml) buttermilk, at room
   temperature
½ cup (115 g) melted coconut oil
2 large eggs, at room temperature
2 teaspoons vanilla extract
1 cup (250 ml) boiling water

1. Preheat the oven to 160°C (320°F) fan forced. Grease two 18 cm (7 inch) round cake tins with cooking oil spray and line with baking paper.

2. Using an electric mixer fitted with the paddle attachment, whisk the flour, sugar, cocoa, bicarbonate of soda, salt and coffee, if using, until combined.

3. Add the buttermilk, coconut oil, eggs and vanilla and mix on medium speed until well combined. Reduce the speed, carefully add the boiling water and mix until well combined.

4. Divide the batter between the cake tins. Bake for 45–50 minutes or until a skewer inserted into the centre of the cakes comes out clean. Remove from the oven and allow the cakes to cool for about 20 minutes, then remove from the tins and transfer to a wire rack to cool completely.

CHOCOLATE GANACHE

200 ml (7 fl oz) single (pure) cream
400 g (14 oz) good-quality dark or
   milk chocolate, chopped

1. Pour the cream into a small saucepan and bring to a rolling boil (there should be bubbles all over the surface, not just around the edge). Remove from the heat and add the dark or milk chocolate, stirring until there are no lumps.

2. Set the ganache aside overnight at room temperature to thicken.

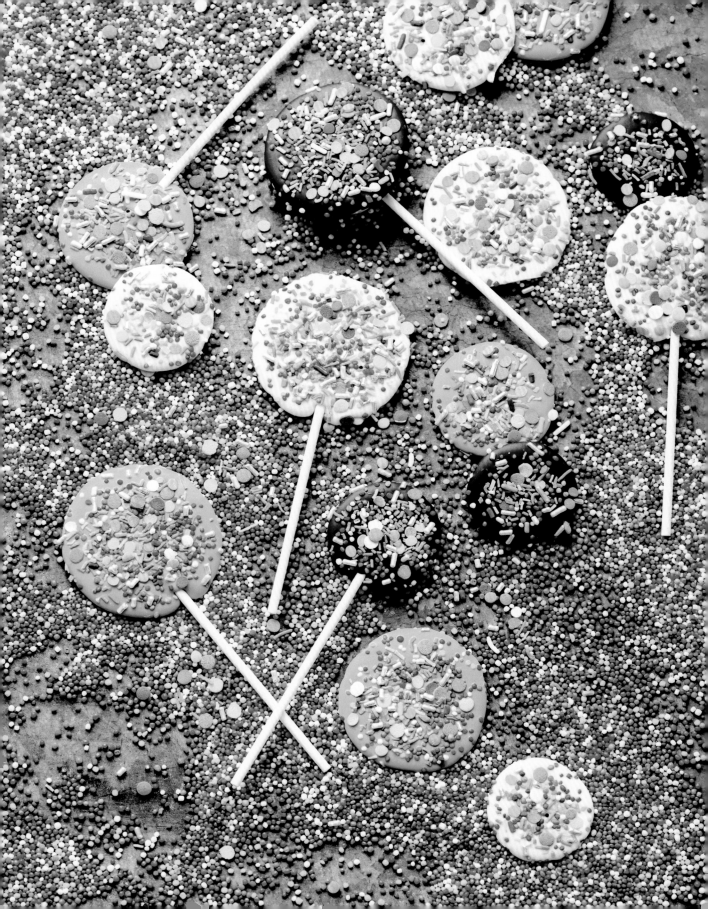

MINT BUTTERCREAM

½ cup (125 g) unsalted butter,
   softened
1½ cups (210 g) icing (confectioners')
   sugar, sifted
1 teaspoon peppermint essence,
   or to taste

1. Using an electric mixer, beat the butter until pale and creamy.
2. Add the icing sugar, one large spoonful at a time, beating constantly until smooth and combined.
3. Add a small amount of the peppermint essence and beat until combined. Continue adding the peppermint essence until you're happy with the taste.

CHOC FRECKLE POPS

300 g (10½ oz) mixture of milk, dark
   and white chocolate, chopped
   (see tips)
Blue oil-based chocolate colouring
   (optional)
Lollipop sticks
Assorted sprinkles

1. Line two baking trays with baking paper. Or to make your job easier, use silicone macaron trays (this will help you to form perfect circular freckles).
2. Melt each type of chocolate separately using either the microwave or double-boiler method (see page 245). Colour the white chocolate with the blue colouring, if using.
3. Working with one tray at a time, drop different-sized spoonfuls of chocolate onto the tray (or pipe chocolate circles using a piping bag). Tap the tray on the bench to form smooth circles. Place a lollipop stick in each circle and cover with some extra chocolate, if needed. Working quickly, generously cover the chocolate circles with sprinkles and tap the tray to help embed the sprinkles in the chocolate.
4. Reheat the chocolate if needed to make the second tray of freckle pops.
5. Set the trays aside in a cool, dark and dry place until the chocolate has set. Transfer the choc freckle pops to an airtight container (you'll have around 30 freckle pops) and save any extra sprinkles for another time.

ASSEMBLY AND DECORATION

1. Working on a cake turntable or lazy Susan, secure the bottom layer of cake onto a cake plate or board with a dollop of buttercream and then gently twist in place. Use an offset spatula to cover the top of the cake with a thick layer of buttercream, spreading it right to the edge.

2. Place the second cake layer on top and gently press down to secure. Using an offset spatula, smooth the excess buttercream so that it very lightly covers the side and gives a smooth edge.

3. Using the offset spatula, gently crumb coat the cake with a thin layer of chocolate ganache (see page 240), gently reheating the ganache to a workable consistency if needed. Chill in the refrigerator for 20 minutes.

4. Apply a final generous layer of ganache all over the cake and use an offset spatula to achieve a swirled, rustic finish.

5. Using the picture on page 71 as a guide, decorate the chocolate cake with the freckle pops.

STORAGE

- The cake is best served at room temperature. It can be refrigerated for up to 5 days or frozen for up to 2 months.
- Store the freckle pops in an airtight container for up to 1 month in a cool, dark and dry place.

Decorating Tips

- You can replace the mint flavouring in the buttercream with vanilla or another flavouring suitable for buttercream.
- I used hundreds and thousands, rainbow jimmies and edible confetti to make the freckle pops.
- If you are using any type of couverture chocolate (my personal favourite), which contains a high cocoa butter content, you will need to temper (also known as 'crystallise') the chocolate (see page 245). This will give the best taste, texture and overall results. Chocolate melts (compound chocolate) will also work well and you won't need to temper the chocolate, so the process will be easy as!

TROPI-COOL PARTY

If you're a cake lover (and I have a sneaking suspicion you are), you might have seen, or even remember, the original pool cake from the 1980 *Australian Women's Weekly Birthday Cake Book*. What a birthday show-stopper! A pool of bright blue or green jelly, surrounded by a chocolate-finger-biscuit picket fence, this cake celebrated the Aussie dream of owning your own backyard swimming pool. It became an Aussie icon in its own right and I reckon it's time we celebrated the vibe and relived that 80s dream!

SERVES 12

SPONGE CAKE

⅔ cup (160 g) unsalted butter, softened

1 cup (220 g) caster sugar

1½ cups (240 g) self-raising flour, sifted

4 eggs, at room temperature, lightly whisked

2 tablespoons hot water

1. Preheat the oven to 160°C (320°F) fan forced. Lightly grease two 20 cm (8 inch) round cake tins and line the base of each tin with baking paper.

2. Using an electric mixer, beat the butter and sugar until light, pale and creamy. Add 2 tablespoons of the flour, then gradually add the eggs, beating well after each addition.

3. Gently fold in the remaining flour and the hot water.

4. Divide the batter evenly between the cake tins. Bake for 20–25 minutes or until the centre of each cake springs back when lightly pressed. Leave in the tins for 5 minutes before transferring to a wire rack to cool completely. Cover and set aside until needed.

VANILLA BUTTERCREAM

2 cups (500 g) salted butter, softened

2 cups (280 g) icing (confectioners') sugar, sifted

2 teaspoons vanilla bean paste

Turquoise gel food colouring

1. Using an electric mixer, beat the butter on high speed for 10–15 minutes or until doubled in size and very pale in colour.

2. Add the icing sugar, in one-third increments, and beat until incorporated and fluffy.

3. Add the vanilla and beat in the food colouring, a few drops at a time, until the buttercream reaches the desired shade.

ASSEMBLY AND DECORATION

85 g (3 oz) packet blue jelly,
   prepared according to the packet
   instructions, chilled
1 packet liquorice allsorts
Black liquorice rope
8 musk sticks
1 roll gummy rope
8 gummy rings
1 fruit Roll-Ups
1 green Pocky stick
40 g (1½ oz) white fondant
2 chocolate-filled wafer rolls
50 g (1¾ oz) white chocolate melts
Green oil-based or powdered
   chocolate colouring
6 Maltesers
1 cocktail umbrella
1 Honey Jumbles biscuit
Writing icing in assorted colours
1 handful Tiny Teddy biscuits
1 Iced VoVo biscuit
1¼ cups (110 g) desiccated coconut
Green food colouring

STORAGE

The cake can be refrigerated
for up to 3 days. It is best
served at room temperature.
Decorations can soften or
dry out once chilled, so you
may want to add the finishing
decorations (such as the jelly
and any biscuits) when you're
ready to serve your cake.

1. Working on a cake turntable or lazy Susan, secure the bottom layer of cake onto a cake plate or board with a dollop of buttercream and then gently twist in place. Use an offset spatula to cover the top of the cake with a layer of buttercream, about 1 cm (½ inch) thick, spreading it right to the edge.

2. Place the second layer of cake on top and gently press down to secure. Using an 18 cm (7 inch) plate or cake tin as a guide, cut a 2 cm (¾ inch) deep hole in the top of the cake to form a pool (eat the offcuts!). Spread buttercream over the base and side of the hole.

3. Using an offset spatula and a cake scraper, gently crumb coat the entire cake with a thin layer of buttercream (see page 240). Carefully smooth the side until the desired finish is achieved. Chill in the refrigerator for 20 minutes.

4. Apply another layer of buttercream to the chilled cake and use the cake scraper and offset spatula to smooth the side and top (see page 241) — or you may choose a more rustic finish.

5. Use a spoon to gently break up the jelly. Using the picture on page 77 as a guide, spoon the jelly into the hole in the top of the cake.

6. Slice the liquorice allsorts into tiles, reserving one whole liquorice allsort for the diving board. Arrange the tiles around the top of the cake.

7. Make the ladder by slicing the liquorice rope and pressing it onto the cake.

8. Cut the musk sticks to size and press them onto the side of the cake. Cut the gummy rope to size, thread a gummy ring through each piece and attach them to the side of the cake.

9. Slice the fruit Roll-Ups and wrap it around the Pocky stick to make a flag. Insert it into the cake.

10. Use the fondant to secure the wafer rolls to the cake plate or board. Melt the white chocolate using either the microwave or double-boiler method (see page 245). Tint with green chocolate colouring. Use the chocolate to pipe leaf shapes onto a sheet of baking paper and allow them to set. Stick the Maltesers onto the leaves with the chocolate, then very carefully secure the leaves onto the trunks with more chocolate.

11. Insert the cocktail umbrella and assemble the diving board. Use the writing icing to add the details to the Tiny Teddy biscuits and position them on the cake, along with the pool floats, as shown.

12. Put the coconut in a resealable plastic bag and add several drops of green colouring. Seal the bag, then shake the bag and massage the coconut until it reaches the desired shade. Sprinkle the coloured coconut around the base of the cake.

BYRON BAY KOMBI CAKE

The VW Kombi campervan is synonymous with the youth rite of passage that is 'travelling around Australia'. The heavily laden van generally blows a gasket at the end of day two of the six-month trip, pretty much at the turn-off for Byron Bay. The Kombi gives us the freedom of being able to travel with all of life's necessities (even the kitchen sink), and the bliss of enjoying a beer and barbecue from the convenience of 'home' at sunset. I've chosen a Byron-ish banana bread as the base cake, but this will work with almost any flavour Kombi-nation.

SERVES 30

BANANA BREAD

2½ cups (400 g) self-raising flour

1½ teaspoons bicarbonate of soda (baking soda)

½ teaspoon salt

¾ cup (185 ml) olive oil

1½ cups (240 g) brown sugar

¼ cup (80 g) honey

1½ tablespoons ground cinnamon

3 teaspoons vanilla extract

3 large eggs

5 large ripe bananas, mashed

¼ cup (65 g) plain yoghurt

2¼ cups (250 g) walnuts, chopped

1. Preheat the oven to 160°C (320°F) fan forced. Grease a tall 13.5 x 23.5 cm (5¼ x 9¼ inch) loaf tin and line the base and sides with baking paper.

2. Put the flour, bicarbonate of soda and salt in a bowl and mix to combine.

3. Whisk the olive oil and brown sugar in a large bowl, breaking up any lumps. Add the honey, cinnamon and vanilla, whisking until smooth. Add the eggs, one at a time, and beat until fully incorporated, then stir in the banana, yoghurt and walnuts. Gently fold in the flour mixture until combined.

4. Pour the batter into the loaf tin. Bake for 60–65 minutes or until a skewer inserted into the centre of the cake comes out clean. Briefly cool in the tin, then turn onto a wire rack to cool.

VANILLA CREAM CHEESE FROSTING

600 g (1 lb 5 oz) cream cheese, softened

50 g (1¾ oz) unsalted butter, softened

1 teaspoon vanilla bean paste

150 g (5½ oz) icing (confectioners') sugar, sifted

1 tablespoon lemon juice

1. Using an electric mixer, beat the cream cheese, butter and vanilla until fluffy.

2. Gradually add the icing sugar while beating. Add the lemon juice and beat until fluffy.

ASSEMBLY AND DECORATION

Rainbow sour straps

6 liquorice allsorts

1 rainbow fruit Roll-Ups

Black liquorice rope

200 g (7 oz) white chocolate melts

Blue oil-based or powdered
 chocolate colouring

4 round chocolate-coated biscuits

4 sugar emojis (optional)

Edible silver paint

2 round fruit gums

2 mini sugar flowers

2 green Pocky sticks

150 g (5½ oz) biscuit crumbs
 (see tips)

Decorating Tips

- For a nut-free cake, omit the walnuts from the banana bread.
- I found the emojis and flowers in the supermarket baking aisle.
- I used store-bought Anzac biscuits to make the biscuit crumbs. Crush them with a food processor or rolling pin.
- You can use edible lustre dust mixed with cake decorators' rose spirit instead of the edible silver paint.

STORAGE

The cake can be refrigerated for up to 5 days. It is best served at room temperature. Decorations can soften once chilled, so you may want to finish decorating your cake just before serving.

1. Use a long, thin knife to divide the banana bread into two even layers. Secure the bottom layer onto a large board or serving plate with a dollop of frosting and then gently twist in place. Use an offset spatula to apply a layer of frosting to sandwich the layers. Place the second layer of banana bread on top and gently press down to secure.

2. Carve the banana bread to resemble the curved shape of a Kombi Van.

3. Use an offset spatula to cover the van with frosting and smooth with a cake scraper until the desired finish is achieved. You may need to put some extra frosting on top to accentuate the curved roof.

4. Cut some of the rainbow sour straps to size and, using the picture on page 80 as a guide, decorate the sides, front and back of the van.

5. Cut the liquorice allsorts into tiles. Stick the pieces in place to make the windows on the sides of the van.

6. Cut the fruit Roll-Ups to make the front and back windscreens and the front passenger windows. Cut some of the liquorice rope to make the side vents. Stick the pieces in place, using a dab of frosting, if needed.

7. To make the bunting for the front and back of the van, cut two long strips from the rainbow sour straps and stick them in place. Cut another sour strap into small triangles and stick them in place.

8. Melt the white chocolate using either the microwave or double-boiler method (see page 245). Tint half the melted chocolate with blue chocolate colouring to the desired shade.

9. To make the surfboard, spread most of the white chocolate evenly over a sheet of baking paper so it is about 2–3 mm (1/16–1/8 inch) thick. Dollop the blue chocolate over the white chocolate and tap or shake to level. Use a skewer to create a swirled effect. Cut out a surfboard shape with a small knife before the chocolate sets completely. Carefully separate the board from the excess chocolate. Allow to set completely.

10. Use the left-over chocolate or frosting to stick the chocolate biscuits onto the sides of the van to make the wheels. Add the sugar emojis, if using.

11. Cut the peace sign, wiper blades and front grille from the liquorice rope. Use the edible silver paint to add the details. Paint on the window details. Paint the fruit gums silver. Stick the decorations in place on the front of the van, along with the sugar flowers.

12. Place the Pocky sticks on top of the van and add the chocolate surfboard.

13. Sprinkle the biscuit crumbs around the base of the van.

Sandwich the cakes with a layer of cream cheese frosting, then carve the top to resemble the curved shape of a Kombi Van.

Cover the top and sides of the Kombi Van with a thick layer of cream cheese frosting.

Use a cake scraper to smooth the frosting until you're happy with the way it looks.

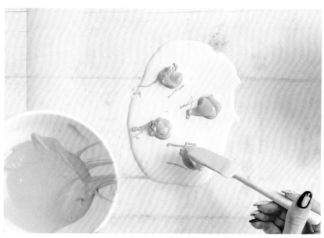

Dollop blobs of the melted blue chocolate onto the melted white chocolate on a sheet of baking paper.

Gently drag a bamboo skewer through the melted chocolate to create a swirled effect.

Carefully cut out a surfboard shape from the chocolate before it has set completely.

WOMBAT CAKE

Curious Aussie fact: one of the wombat's primary defences is its super-tough backside, which it uses to defend its burrow. While they might look cute and cuddly, these brave marsupials are strong enough to protect themselves against intruders on their home soil, and have been known to bowl people over with... their bum. Be afraid. Be very afraid. This is an animal trained for combat. A combat wombat, if you will. Another curious fact about the wombat bottom: its poo is cube shaped. If you're looking for a more peace-keeping wombat, feel free to leave off the accessories. Wombats are a unique Aussie icon, whatever they wear.

SERVES 30

CARAMEL MUDCAKES

400 g (14 oz) unsalted butter, chopped

400 g (14 oz) good-quality white chocolate, chopped

2 cups (500 ml) hot water

2 tablespoons golden syrup

1 tablespoon vanilla extract

2 cups (320 g) dark brown sugar

4 eggs, at room temperature

4 cups (640 g) self-raising flour

1. Preheat the oven to 160°C (320°F) fan forced. Grease two 20 cm (8 inch) ovenproof glass bowls.

2. Combine the butter, chocolate, hot water, golden syrup and vanilla in a saucepan. Cook over low heat, whisking constantly, until smooth and well combined. Remove from the heat and set aside until lukewarm.

3. Meanwhile, use electric beaters to whisk the brown sugar and eggs in a large mixing bowl until pale and creamy. Whisk in the chocolate mixture until well combined. Add the flour and whisk until combined.

4. Pour the batter into the bowls. Bake the cakes for 55 minutes or until a skewer inserted into the centre comes out almost clean. (The centre of the mudcakes will still be quite sticky — almost gooey — but will come together once cooled.) Leave the cakes to cool in the bowls for at least 1 hour. Do not turn out the cakes until they have completely cooled, otherwise they may fall apart. Cover the cooled cakes with plastic wrap or a clean, damp tea towel and set aside until needed.

WHIPPED CHOCOLATE GANACHE

400 ml (14 fl oz) single (pure) cream

800 g (1 lb 12 oz) good-quality milk chocolate, chopped

1. Pour the cream into a small saucepan and bring to a rolling boil (there should be bubbles all over the surface, not just around the edge). Remove from the heat and add the chopped chocolate, stirring until there are no lumps. Set aside to cool to room temperature.

2. Use an electric mixer to beat the ganache on high speed until it lightens in colour and becomes thick and spoonable.

ASSEMBLY AND DECORATION

1 store-bought mini sponge roll

2 pink Honey Jumbles biscuits

2 Maltesers

1 TeeVee Snacks biscuit

18 red liquorice twists

Black liquorice rope

100 g (3½ oz) green fondant

100 g (3½ oz) brown fondant

Cornflour, for rolling

16 slivered almonds

Sunglasses or protective goggles
   (see tips)

500 g (1 lb 2 oz) desiccated coconut

Green food colouring

6 Fantales

STORAGE

The cake is best served at room temperature. It can be made ahead and refrigerated for up to 1 week. Decorations can soften once chilled, so you may want to decorate the cake just before serving.

1. Cut a concave section out of one of the cakes as shown. Reserve the offcut.

2. Secure the uncut cake onto a large board with a dollop of the chocolate ganache. Spread some more ganache on the cut side of the other cake and secure it in place on the board. Cut the cake offcut into two pieces to make the front legs. Cut the sponge roll to size to make the back legs. Secure the legs in place with ganache.

3. Using an offset spatula and a cake scraper, gently crumb coat the cake with a thin layer of ganache (see page 240), reheating the ganache if needed. Carefully smooth the ganache until the desired finish is achieved. Chill in the refrigerator for 20 minutes.

4. Apply another layer of ganache to the chilled cake (a rustic finish is just fine!) and use a fork to create 'fur'.

5. Cut off the bottom third of each Honey Jumbles biscuit and insert them into the top of the wombat's head to make ears. Press the Maltesers and the TeeVee Snacks biscuit in place for the wombat's eyes and nose.

6. To make the wombat's stash of fire cracker sticks, lay the red liquorice twists across the wombat's back. Cut the black liquorice rope into a thin strap and lay it across the red liquorice, securing the ends into the cake. Use a little ganache on the underside of the black liquorice to help it stick.

7. Shape the brown and green fondant into several lumps and roll out on a board dusted with cornflour, until a blended effect is achieved. Using a sharp knife, cut the fondant into a bandana shape and drape it over the wombat's body.

8. Insert the slivered almonds into the wombat's paws to make claws. Position the wombat's sunglasses above the eyes.

9. Put the coconut in a resealable plastic bag and add several drops of green colouring. Seal the bag, then shake the bag and massage the coconut until it reaches the desired shade. Spread the coconut around the cake. Arrange the Fantales 'droppings' near the wombat's rear area.

Decorating Tips

- You can prepare the ganache using the microwave. Combine the chocolate and cream in a microwave-safe bowl and microwave on High in 1-minute intervals, stirring for 2 minutes in between, until there are no lumps. I use a stick blender to stir the cream and melted chocolate together as it's much quicker and easier to ensure an even consistency.
- You can use sliced chocolate buttons instead of the slivered almonds for the claws.
- I purchased the sunglasses from a discount store and unscrewed the arms.

Leave the mudcakes in the bowls until they have completely cooled — the centres will be quite sticky and the hot cakes may fall apart.

Use the cake offcut and a sponge roll to make the wombat's legs, and attach them with some of the ganache.

The ganache doesn't need to be completely smooth — use a fork to rough it up so it looks like fur.

Make the wombat's camo bandana by rolling lumps of brown and green fondant together.

PICK 'N' MIX CAKE

Who can resist the nostalgic excitement and freedom of choice of the sweetshop Pick 'n' Mix? Pick your choice of lollies, scoop them into your paper bag, and pay for them by weight. Then it's a lucky dip when you reach into that bag of treasure. The rainbow of colours in the display alone makes my heart sing with anticipatory joy! With this recipe, now we can have it all: lollies AND cake. I feel as reckless as a kid in a candy store.

SERVES 16—20

FUNFETTI SPONGE CAKE

240 g (8½ oz) unsalted butter, softened
1½ cups (330 g) caster sugar
2¼ cups (360 g) self-raising flour, sifted
6 eggs, at room temperature, lightly whisked
¼ cup (60 ml) hot water
½ cup (90 g) rainbow sprinkles (see tips)

1. Preheat the oven to 160°C (320°F) fan forced. Lightly grease three 20 cm (8 inch) round cake tins and line the base of each tin with baking paper.

2. Using an electric mixer, beat the butter and sugar until light, pale and creamy. Add ¼ cup of the flour, then gradually add the eggs, beating well after each addition.

3. Gently fold in the remaining flour and the hot water. Gently stir in the sprinkles until just combined.

4. Divide the mixture evenly among the cake tins. Bake for 30 minutes or until the centre of each cake springs back when lightly pressed. Leave the cakes in the tins for 5 minutes before transferring to a wire rack to cool completely. Cover and set aside until needed.

BUBBLEGUM SWISS MERINGUE BUTTERCREAM

1½ cups (330 g) caster sugar
8 large egg whites
2 cups (500 g) unsalted butter, softened
1—2 teaspoons bubblegum flavouring (see tips)
Turquoise or teal gel food colouring

1. Put the sugar and egg whites in a heatproof glass bowl. Set the bowl over a pan of gently simmering water and whisk until the sugar has dissolved and the mixture is slightly warm to the touch. Remove from the heat.

2. Using an electric mixer fitted with the whisk attachment, beat on high speed until the mixture has formed stiff and glossy peaks (about 10—15 minutes).

3. Add the butter in three batches, beating until incorporated after each addition. Add the bubblegum flavouring, to taste, and beat until fluffy. Mix in the food colouring until the desired shade is reached. Cover the bowl with plastic wrap and set aside in a cool place until needed.

ASSEMBLY AND DECORATION

50 g (1¾ oz) white chocolate, chopped
1 thick wooden skewer or wooden cake dowel
1 party lolly bag or sweet packet
Sticky tape
Assorted lollies, such as liquorice allsorts, sour worms, sour straps, jellybeans, sour bears, banana lollies, musk sticks, conversation hearts, gummy spearmint leaves, chocolate freckles, Fruit Tingles
Rainbow sprinkles

STORAGE

This cake can be stored in an airtight container at room temperature for 2 days, or refrigerated for up to 4 days. Remove it from the fridge at least 1 hour before serving.

1. Working on a cake turntable or lazy Susan, secure the bottom layer of cake onto a cake board or plate with a dollop of buttercream and then gently twist in place. Use an offset spatula to cover the top of the cake with a 5 mm (¼ inch) layer of buttercream, spreading it right to the edge.

2. Place the second cake layer on top and use the spatula and a cake scraper to gently crumb coat the side of the cake with a thin layer of buttercream (see page 240). Repeat the layering process until the last cake layer is added. Carefully smooth the side until the desired finish is achieved. Chill the cake in the refrigerator for 20 minutes.

3. Apply a final thick layer of buttercream all over the cake and use the cake scraper and offset spatula to smooth the top and side (see page 241).

4. Melt the chocolate using either the microwave or double-boiler method (see page 245). Cool until the chocolate is a spreadable consistency.

5. Push the skewer into the centre of the cake and place the lolly bag on top, securing it to the skewer with sticky tape inside the bag.

6. Spread a blob of chocolate onto one of the lollies and, starting at the base, stick it to the skewer. Continue adding the lollies in this way, working your way upwards until the skewer is completely covered. You will need to work in stages to allow the chocolate to set a little before adding more lollies. Gently reheat the bowl of chocolate if it becomes too firm. Check that none of the skewer is exposed and add some more lollies, if needed.

7. Arrange the remaining lollies over the top and side of the cake so that it looks like the lollies are flowing out of the lolly bag. Finish by scattering the cake with some rainbow sprinkles.

Decorating Tips

- For an even taller cake, use three 15 cm (6 inch) cake tins.
- Use rainbow jimmies or the confetti variety of sprinkles in the cake batter. Regular hundreds and thousands will 'bleed' and lose their colour when mixed into the batter.
- I use Roberts Confectionery bubblegum flavouring. You could replace it with 1 teaspoon of vanilla bean paste or any other buttercream flavouring, such as raspberry or caramel.
- I like to use Wilton and AmeriColor brands of gel food colouring.
- If you want the chocolate to cool quickly, put it in the refrigerator, stirring it every minute or so to prevent it from setting.

Cover the first cake layer with a layer of buttercream, spreading it right to the edge, then add the second cake layer.

Repeat the layering process, using a thin layer of buttercream to crumb coat the side of the cake as you go.

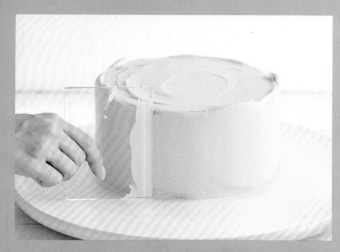

Use a cake scraper held upright against the side of the cake to give the side a smooth finish.

Use a large offset spatula to pull the excess icing in towards the centre of the cake, then smooth the top.

Spread a blob of white chocolate on each lolly and stick it to the skewer, starting from the base.

Arrange the remaining lollies on the top and over the side of the cake and finish with a scattering of rainbow sprinkles.

JAW-SOME CAKE

The release of the movie *Jaws* in 1975 is the exact moment in history that EVERYTHING changed for sharks. Will the great white ever forgive Steven Spielberg for such a gross misrepresentation of its happy-go-lucky character? Couldn't he have chosen a giant flounder as his villain? I know humans aren't the preferred prey of the shark, but I couldn't help myself when it came to this blockbuster of a cake. Just when you thought it was safe to go back in the kitchen...

SERVES 16

DARK CHOCOLATE SEA SALT CAKE

Cooking oil spray
½ cup (90 g) chopped dark
   chocolate
½ cup (115 g) coconut oil
1¼ cups (200 g) self-raising flour
¾ cup (165 g) caster sugar
¼ cup (30 g) cocoa powder
½ teaspoon bicarbonate of soda
   (baking soda)
½ teaspoon sea salt
3 large eggs, at room temperature
¾ cup (185 ml) milk, at room
   temperature
1 teaspoon vanilla extract

1. Preheat the oven to 160°C (320°F) fan forced. Grease a Dolly Varden cake tin with cooking oil spray.

2. Melt the chocolate and coconut oil using either the microwave or double-boiler method (see page 245). Stir until combined. Set the mixture aside to cool to room temperature.

3. Using an electric mixer fitted with the paddle attachment, gently fold the dry ingredients together until combined.

4. With the mixer on low speed, slowly add the chocolate mixture to the dry ingredients. Beat in the eggs, one at a time, then beat in the milk and vanilla. Mix until combined.

5. Pour the batter into the cake tin. Bake for 50 minutes or until a skewer inserted into the centre of the cake comes out clean. Leave to cool in the tin for at least 1 hour before turning out onto a wire rack to cool completely.

VANILLA BUTTERCREAM

100 g (3½ oz) unsalted butter,
   softened
3 cups (420 g) icing (confectioners')
   sugar, sifted
¼ cup (60 ml) milk
1 teaspoon vanilla extract
Black and red gel food colouring

1. Using an electric mixer, beat the butter until very pale. Gradually add the icing sugar while beating on low speed. Add the milk and vanilla and beat on high speed until fluffy.

2. Transfer half of the buttercream into a bowl and tint it grey by mixing in a small amount of black colouring.

3. Divide the remaining buttercream between two bowls. Tint one bowl red and leave the other bowl uncoloured.

ASSEMBLY AND DECORATION

85 g (3 oz) packet blue jelly
12 strawberries and cream lollies
1 liquorice roll
1 teaspoon cornflour
Action doll arm and legs

1. Prepare the jelly according to the packet instructions, using only two-thirds of the quantity of water. Pour into a bowl and refrigerate for 2–3 hours or until set.

2. Using a long, thin knife, trim the cake so it will sit level. Divide the cake into three even horizontal layers.

3. Working on a cake turntable or lazy Susan, secure the bottom layer of cake onto a cake board or serving plate with a dollop of grey buttercream and then gently twist in place. Use an offset spatula to cover the top of the cake with a layer of buttercream.

4. Place the second cake layer on top and add another layer of buttercream, then place the final cake layer on top.

5. Using an offset spatula and a cake scraper, gently crumb coat the entire cake with a thin layer of grey buttercream (see page 240). Chill in the refrigerator for 20 minutes.

6. Apply a final layer of grey buttercream all over the chilled cake and use the cake scraper to smooth the side and top (see page 241).

7. Use a small offset spatula to apply the uncoloured buttercream to the underside of the shark's head and carefully smooth it out.

8. Repeat with the red buttercream to create the inside of the shark's mouth.

9. To create the shark's teeth, use scissors or a small, sharp knife to remove the red section from the strawberries and cream lollies. Cut the remaining white section into the shape of teeth. Press onto the red buttercream to form a row of teeth. Using the picture on page 92 as a guide, blend the white buttercream into the grey buttercream using an offset spatula.

10. Cut two pieces of the liquorice roll to make the shark's eyes and press them into the head.

11. Lightly dust a clean finger with cornflour and gently poke it into the frosting to form two nostril holes.

12. Use a spoon to break up the blue jelly and scatter it around the cake, using the excess buttercream to secure it to the board. Press the action figure's arm and legs in place to resemble a rather unfortunate shark attack... But really, aren't all shark attacks unfortunate?

STORAGE

The cake is best served at room temperature. It can be refrigerated for up to 5 days.

Decorating Tips

- Cut the cake into two layers or leave it as one whole cake, if you prefer.
- You can pipe a thin outline with uncoloured buttercream to create a guide for applying the buttercream for the shark's mouth. Do the same with the red buttercream for the inside of the mouth.

Apply a final layer of grey buttercream all over the layered cake and use a cake scraper to smooth the side and top.

Use a small offset spatula to apply the uncoloured buttercream to the underside of the shark's head, creating the mouth.

Carefully smooth the uncoloured buttercream over the shark's mouth using a small cake scraper.

Use the small offset spatula to apply the red buttercream to create the inside of the shark's mouth.

Cut off the red section of the strawberries and cream lollies, then shape the white section into teeth.

Press the shark's teeth into the red buttercream around the inside of the mouth to create a row of teeth.

THE BIG PINEAPPLE

Our first heritage-listed cake! The Big Pineapple is emblematic of our rather peculiar national love of giant outdoor cultural objects. (Think the Big Merino, the Big Galah, and the slightly menacing Big Prawn... not one for the seafood-timid.) The real Big Pineapple is a tourism and food icon on Queensland's Sunshine Coast. Our cake version, however, is iconically tropi-COOL in its own right. It's filled with luscious pineapple curd for extra zing. This recipe makes excellent use of the entire fruit, which should hopefully save you time when it comes to decorating AND supports your local pineapple farmer. No fruit parties quite as hard as the pineapple.

SERVES 14

VANILLA CAKE

2¾ cups (440 g) self-raising flour
¼ teaspoon salt
½ cup (130 g) unsalted butter, softened
100 ml (3½ fl oz) vegetable oil
1⅓ cups (295 g) caster sugar
2 teaspoons vanilla bean paste
4 eggs, at room temperature
1 cup (250 ml) milk, at room temperature

1. Preheat the oven to 160°C (320°F) fan forced. Grease three 15 cm (6 inch) shallow round cake tins and a 15 cm (6 inch) ovenproof bowl.

2. Sift the flour and salt into a bowl.

3. Using an electric mixer, beat the butter, oil, sugar and vanilla until frothy. Add the eggs, one at a time, and mix until combined.

4. Alternately fold in the flour mixture and the milk, in one-third increments. Fold until just combined.

5. Divide the batter among the tins and bowl. Bake the cakes (in batches, if necessary) for 20–30 minutes or until a skewer inserted into the centre comes out clean. Leave to cool slightly before turning out onto wire racks (with the tops facing down) to cool completely. Cover the cold cakes with plastic wrap or a clean, damp tea towel and set aside until needed.

PINEAPPLE CURD

1 cup (250 ml) pineapple purée (see tips)
2 tablespoons lemon juice
⅓ cup (75 g) caster sugar
3 egg yolks
2 tablespoons cornflour
1 pinch salt
¼ cup (60 g) butter, chopped

1. Add the pineapple purée, lemon juice, sugar, egg yolks, cornflour and salt to a saucepan and whisk to combine. Whisk constantly over medium heat until the mixture thickens (this happens just as it's about to come to the boil). Remove from the heat. Add the butter and whisk until melted.

2. Transfer the pineapple curd to a jar and refrigerate until thickened and cooled before using to fill the cake.

VANILLA BEAN SWISS MERINGUE BUTTERCREAM

1½ cups (330 g) caster sugar
8 large egg whites
2 cups (500 g) unsalted butter, softened
1 teaspoon vanilla bean paste
Yellow gel food colouring

1. Put the sugar and egg whites in a heatproof glass bowl. Set the bowl over a pan of gently simmering water and whisk until the sugar has dissolved and the mixture is slightly warm to the touch. Remove from the heat.

2. Using an electric mixer fitted with the whisk attachment, beat on high speed until the mixture has formed stiff and glossy peaks (about 10–15 minutes).

3. Add the butter in three batches, beating until incorporated after each addition. (Don't be alarmed if it appears curdled — it will become light and fluffy with continued whipping.) Add the vanilla and beat until fluffy.

4. Transfer one-third of the buttercream to a bowl. Beat the yellow colouring into the remaining buttercream until the desired shade is reached. Cover the bowls with plastic wrap and set aside in a cool place.

ASSEMBLY AND DECORATION

1 wooden cake dowel
1 small pineapple top, washed
1 small cardboard circle (about the size of the bottom of the pineapple top)

1. Working on a cake turntable or lazy Susan, secure the bottom layer of cake onto a cake board or plate with a dollop of buttercream and then gently twist in place.

2. Fill a piping bag with buttercream and pipe a 1 cm (½ inch) barrier around the edge of the cake to create a well. Fill the well with pineapple curd and gently place the second cake layer on top. Add the buttercream and pineapple curd as for the first layer, then repeat for the third layer.

3. Using an offset spatula and a cake scraper, gently crumb coat the side of the cake with a thick layer of buttercream (see page 240). Level the top of the bowl cake and gently place upside down on top of the layered cake. Crumb coat the top of the cake. Chill in the refrigerator for 20 minutes.

4. Place the yellow buttercream in a piping bag fitted with a star nozzle. Working from the bottom, pipe the buttercream all over the cake.

5. Push the cake dowel into the bottom of the pineapple top until the length of dowel remaining is the same height as the cake. Push the dowel into the cardboard circle, then gently push the dowel into the cake until secure.

STORAGE

- The assembled cake can be refrigerated for up to 5 days. It is best served at room temperature.
- The pineapple curd can be refrigerated in a sealed glass jar for up to 2 weeks.

Decorating Tips

- Use a stick blender or food processor to purée fresh or frozen pineapple for the pineapple curd.
- If your cake appears unstable when you're assembling it, refrigerate it before adding each layer to help it firm up (especially if it's a hot day).
- I used a Wilton '1M' metal tip to pipe the yellow buttercream.

Pipe a barrier of buttercream around the edge of the cake to create a well for the pineapple curd.

Gently place the second cake layer on top of the buttercream and pineapple curd filling.

Once you have added the final layer of buttercream and pineapple curd, place the upside-down bowl cake on top.

Starting from the bottom, pipe the yellow buttercream all over the cake – this is much easier to do when you're working on a cake turntable.

Push the cake dowel into the pineapple top and add the cardboard circle to help protect the cake.

Gently push the pineapple top all the way down through the layers of cake and filling.

DAME EDNA KOALA

Dame Edna Everage, self-proclaimed housewife megastar, is one of Australia's most internationally recognised characters, known for her waves of 'wisteria' hair, bejewelled glasses and animated greeting: 'Hello, possums!' She is the alter-ego of comedy genius Barry Humphries and has made generations of Aussies laugh and squirm. This cheeky koala is modelling her enviable glasses.

SERVES 16

VIOLET VELVET CAKE

2 cups (320 g) plain flour
1 cup (220 g) caster sugar
1 teaspoon baking powder
¼ teaspoon bicarbonate of soda
 (baking soda)
¼ teaspoon salt
⅔ cup (170 ml) vegetable oil
2 teaspoons vanilla extract or
 1 teaspoon vanilla bean paste
2 large eggs, at room temperature
1 cup (250 ml) buttermilk, at room
 temperature
Violet gel food colouring

1. Preheat the oven to 160°C (320°F) fan forced. Grease a 23 cm (9 inch) ovenproof bowl and line a cupcake tray with one cupcake case.

2. Sift the flour, sugar, baking powder, bicarbonate of soda and salt together.

3. Using an electric mixer, whisk the oil and vanilla at high speed until light and fluffy. Whisk in the eggs, one at a time.

4. Gently incorporate the dry ingredients in three batches, alternating with the buttermilk in two batches. Add the food colouring until the desired shade is reached and gently mix until just combined, being careful not to over-mix.

5. Fill the cupcake case with batter and pour the rest into the ovenproof bowl. Bake the cupcake for 10–15 minutes and the bowl cake for 45–50 minutes or until a skewer inserted into the centre comes out clean. Leave the cake to cool in the bowl for 1 hour, then turn onto a wire rack, upside down, to cool completely. Cover and set aside until needed.

VANILLA BEAN SWISS MERINGUE BUTTERCREAM

1½ cups (330 g) caster sugar
8 large egg whites
2 cups (500 g) unsalted butter,
 softened
1 teaspoon vanilla bean paste
Pink and violet gel food colouring

1. Put the sugar and egg whites in a heatproof glass bowl. Set the bowl over a pan of gently simmering water and whisk until the sugar has dissolved and the mixture is slightly warm to the touch. Remove from the heat.

2. Using an electric mixer fitted with the whisk attachment, beat on high speed until the mixture has formed stiff and glossy peaks (about 10–15 minutes).

3. Add the butter in three batches, beating until incorporated after each addition. Add the vanilla and beat until fluffy. Tint half of the buttercream pink and the other half violet. Cover and set aside in a cool place.

ASSEMBLY AND DECORATION

½ cup (150 g) lemon curd (page 246
    or store-bought)
4 toothpicks
Black liquorice rope
1 liquorice roll
200 g (7 oz) dark chocolate melts
**Black oil-based or powdered
    chocolate colouring (optional)**
Silver cachous
10 gummy jubes, halved lengthways
2 liquorice allsorts

1. Using a long, thin knife, trim the bowl cake and cupcake so they're level. Cut the cupcake in half vertically to make two ears. Cut the bowl cake in half horizontally to make two layers.

2. Working on a cake turntable or lazy Susan, secure the bottom layer of cake onto a cake board or serving plate with a dollop of pink buttercream and then gently twist in place. Use an offset spatula to cover the top of the cake with a layer of pink buttercream, spreading it right to the edge.

3. Fill a piping bag with pink buttercream and pipe a 1 cm (½ inch) barrier around the edge of the cake to create a 'dam' (see page 239). Fill the 'dam' with lemon curd and gently place the second cake layer on top.

4. Using an offset spatula, gently crumb coat the cake with pink buttercream (see page 240). Spread the buttercream over the cupcake ears. Attach the ears to the sides of the head, with the top of the cupcakes facing forwards, and secure with toothpicks. Chill the cake in the refrigerator for 20 minutes.

5. Apply a final layer of pink buttercream to the chilled cake and use a small cake scraper to smooth the buttercream (see page 241).

6. Slice the liquorice rope and the liquorice roll to make the eyes, nose and mouth. Gently embed them into the cake.

7. Apply a small amount of violet buttercream to the centre of the ears.

8. Fill a piping bag fitted with a star nozzle with the violet buttercream. Pipe waves of hair onto the cake.

9. Melt the dark chocolate using either the microwave or double-boiler method (see page 245). Tint with black chocolate colouring, if using. Spoon the chocolate into a piping bag with the tip cut off at 2–3 mm (⅛–¹⁄₁₆ inch). Trace the glasses template opposite onto a sheet of baking paper. Pipe the outline of the glasses and then fill in with more chocolate. Apply a second layer of chocolate if needed. Before the chocolate sets, quickly decorate the glasses with the silver cachous. Leave the glasses to set completely (you can speed this up by placing them in the freezer or refrigerator for 10–15 minutes).

10. Gently embed the chocolate glasses onto the cake, using some left-over buttercream to stick them if needed. Adorn the cake with the gummy jubes, and use the liquorice allsorts for earrings.

Decorating Tip

- If you don't wish to make the glasses out of chocolate, look for Dame Edna tribute sunglasses in costume stores and online. Simply unscrew the arms when using on the cake. They can be put back together afterwards.

THE GLAMINGTON

What do you get when a lamington dresses up for a big night out? A glamington, of course! The lamington, our very own, Queensland-born, sponge-cube-rolled-in-coconut sensation, is magicked into an elegant layered cake with this fairytale recipe. As a variation, use dark chocolate melts instead of white in the ganache, or make the cakes chocolate and tint the ganache with pink food colouring instead. Whatever you do, don't forget to celebrate with a slice of this retro beauty on the 21st of July, because that is officially National Lamington Day.

SERVES 12—16

VANILLA CAKE

½ cup (130 g) unsalted butter, softened
1 cup (220 g) caster sugar
1 teaspoon vanilla bean paste
3 large eggs, at room temperature
2⅓ cups (375 g) self-raising flour
1 cup (250 ml) milk, at room temperature
1 pinch salt

1. Preheat the oven to 160°C (320°F) fan forced. Grease three 15 cm (6 inch) shallow round cake tins.

2. Using an electric mixer fitted with the paddle attachment, cream the butter, sugar and vanilla until light and fluffy. Add the eggs, one at a time, and mix until thoroughly combined.

3. Gently incorporate the flour in three batches, alternating with the milk in two batches. Add the salt and mix until just combined, being careful not to over-mix.

4. Divide the batter among the cake tins. Bake for about 20–30 minutes or until a skewer inserted into the centre of each cake comes out clean. Leave the cakes to cool in the tins for 15 minutes before turning onto a wire rack, upside down, to cool completely. Cover and set aside.

WHITE CHOCOLATE GANACHE

1 cup (250 ml) single (pure) cream
500 g (1 lb 2 oz) white chocolate melts
Pink gel food colouring

1. Pour the cream into a small saucepan and bring to a rolling boil (there should be bubbles all over the surface, not just around the edge). Remove from the heat and add the chocolate, stirring until there are no lumps.

2. Stir in the pink colouring until the desired shade is reached.

3. Set the ganache aside until it cools and thickens slightly. If needed, briefly chill it in the fridge (for about 5–10 minutes), then stir again until smooth. Once the ganache has reached the right consistency, transfer it to a wide, shallow dish.

ASSEMBLY AND DECORATION

3 cups (255 g) fine desiccated
  coconut
300 ml (10½ fl oz) single (pure)
  cream
125 g (4½ oz) fresh raspberries

1. Put the coconut in a wide, shallow dish. Gently dip one of the cake layers into the pink ganache, ensuring even coverage, then dip into the coconut. Place the cake on a plate and refrigerate for 30 minutes or until set. Repeat with the remaining cake layers.

2. Using an electric mixer fitted with the whisk attachment, whip the cream until stiff peaks form.

3. Place the bottom cake layer on a cake stand or plate. Dollop a generous amount of whipped cream on top and spread it over the cake. Stud the cream with the raspberries. Spread a little more whipped cream on top to help secure the next cake layer.

4. Add the second cake layer and top with more cream and raspberries. Gently place the third cake layer on top.

Decorating Tips

- To prepare the ganache using the microwave, put the white chocolate melts in a microwave-safe bowl. Pour the cream into another microwave-safe container and heat for 30–40 seconds or just until it starts to boil. Pour the cream over the white chocolate, making sure that most of the white chocolate is covered. Set aside for 5 minutes, then stir in a gentle, circular motion until the white chocolate has melted and the mixture is smooth. If needed, microwave for another 10 seconds at a time, stirring gently until smooth.

- You can also cook the cake batter in one 15 cm (6 inch) deep cake tin. Increase the baking time to 50–60 minutes. Once the cake is completely cooled, use a long, thin knife to divide it into three even layers.

RAINBOW SERPENT CAKE

The Rainbow Serpent is one of the most well-known Dreamtime creation stories and holds great importance in Aboriginal society. When a rainbow appears in the sky, that's the sign that the Rainbow Serpent is moving from one waterhole to another. This rainbow snake cake will bring joy to any gathering. Embedded with edible jewels and rainbow decoration, it is a truly dazzling sight.

SERVES 30–35

VANILLA CAKE

½ cup (130 g) unsalted butter, softened
1 cup (220 g) caster sugar
1 teaspoon vanilla bean paste
3 large eggs, at room temperature
1 pinch salt
2⅓ cups (375 g) self-raising flour
1 cup (250 ml) milk, at room temperature

1. Preheat the oven to 160°C (320°F) fan forced. Lightly grease a pair of non-stick 25 cm (10 inch) doughnut tins.

2. Using an electric mixer, cream the butter, sugar and vanilla until light and fluffy. Add the eggs, one at a time, beating until combined. Add the salt.

3. Alternately fold in the flour and the milk, in one-third increments. Fold until just combined.

4. Divide the batter between the doughnut tins and smooth the surface with the back of a spoon or spatula. Bake for 20–25 minutes or until a skewer inserted into the centre of the cakes comes out clean. Cool in the tins for 15 minutes, then gently turn out onto a wire rack to cool completely. Cover the cakes with a clean, damp tea towel to prevent them from drying out.

VANILLA BEAN SWISS MERINGUE BUTTERCREAM

1½ cups (330 g) caster sugar
8 large egg whites
2 cups (500 g) unsalted butter, softened
1 teaspoon vanilla bean paste
Blue, pink, green and orange gel food colouring

1. Put the sugar and egg whites in a heatproof glass bowl. Set the bowl over a pan of gently simmering water and whisk until the sugar has dissolved and the mixture is slightly warm to the touch. Remove from the heat.

2. Using an electric mixer fitted with the whisk attachment, beat on high speed until the mixture has formed stiff and glossy peaks (about 10–15 minutes).

3. Add the butter in three batches, beating until incorporated after each addition. Add the vanilla and beat until fluffy.

4. Divide the buttercream among four bowls and tint each portion until the desired shade is reached. Cover and set aside in a cool place.

ASSEMBLY AND DECORATION

350 g (12 oz) packet gummy jubes,
   halved lengthways
3 x 50 g (1¾ oz) packets Smarties
1 rainbow sour strap

1. Carefully slice each cake in half and position the pieces on an 80 x 40 cm (32 x 16 inch) cake board to make a serpent shape, as shown. Use a little of the buttercream to secure the cake pieces to the board.

2. Use a knife to trim the head and tail of the snake, then brush away the excess crumbs.

3. Use an offset spatula to apply a different shade of buttercream to each cake section.

4. Decorate the serpent's body with the halved jubes and the Smarties, using the picture as a guide.

5. Use sharp scissors or a knife to cut the sour strap into the shape of the serpent's tongue and attach it to the cake.

6. Attach small strips of sour strap to two halved black jubes and place on the cake to create the eyes.

STORAGE

The cake is best served at room temperature. It can be refrigerated in an airtight container for up to 5 days.

Decorating Tips

- Doughnut tins are sold in cake decorating stores and through online retailers. Alternatively, use two 25 cm (10 inch) bundt tins.
- You can also use pasteurised egg whites from a carton to make Swiss meringue buttercream. You won't need to whisk the sugar into the egg whites over a pan of simmering water – simply place the sugar and egg whites directly into the mixer.
- You won't need to use all of the jubes or Smarties, but the quantities I've suggested should ensure you have enough sweets of each colour to decorate the serpent as shown.

Wait until the doughnut cakes are completely cool before cutting each cake in half.

Arrange the cake pieces on a large cake board to make the serpent shape and trim the head and tail.

Starting at the tail end, apply a different shade of buttercream to each section of cake.

Decorate the serpent's body with the jubes and Smarties as shown – or create your own design.

ICED VOVO™ TRIFLE

The Iced VoVo is the crochet-loving fashionista of the biscuit world. This pastel beauty was brought to us in 1906 by the American-owned Australian-based biscuit company, Arnott's. In this trifle, we celebrate the iconic flavours of Iced VoVo's sticky raspberry, with soft panels of pink sweetness and a delicate sprinkling of coconut. A trifle is a top dessert because it makes a beautiful table decoration, as well as tasting great. I think this has got to be the prettiest one on the shelf!

SERVES 20

JELLY LAYER

2 x 85 g (3 oz) packets raspberry jelly

1. Prepare one of the packets of jelly according to the packet instructions. Pour the jelly into a large trifle bowl and refrigerate for at least 1 hour.

2. Prepare the second packet of jelly according to the packet instructions, using only half the quantity of water to ensure the jelly sets firm enough to hold its shape when cut. Pour the jelly into a small straight-sided dish and refrigerate for at least 3 hours. Once the jelly has set, cut it into cubes.

RASPBERRY MARSHMALLOW

250 g (9 oz) caster sugar
½ cup (125 ml) water
2 large egg whites
70 ml (2¼ fl oz) warm water
1½ tablespoons powdered gelatine
1 cup (150 g) frozen raspberries, thawed and puréed
1 teaspoon vanilla extract
Pink gel food colouring (optional)
½ cup (45 g) fine desiccated coconut

1. Place the sugar and ½ cup of water in a large heavy-based saucepan. Bring to the boil over high heat, without stirring. Once the syrup reaches 110°C (230°F) on a candy thermometer, use an electric mixer to whip the egg whites into firm peaks. Continue cooking the syrup.

2. Meanwhile, pour the warm water into a small bowl and add the gelatine.

3. When the syrup reaches 120°C (250°F), remove the pan from the heat and gently stir in the gelatine mixture until well combined. With the mixer on the highest speed, continue to whip the egg whites whilst carefully pouring in the hot syrup. Whip until the mixture thickens and increases in volume, but remains pourable. Add the raspberry purée, vanilla and food colouring, if using. Working quickly, pour three-quarters of the marshmallow over the set jelly. Refrigerate for at least 1 hour or until completely set.

4. Pour the extra marshmallow into a small, greased straight-sided dish and refrigerate for at least 1 hour. Once set, cut into cubes and roll in the coconut.

ASSEMBLY AND DECORATION

1 jam sponge roll (see tip)
¾ cup (200 g) thick Greek-style yoghurt
300 ml (10½ fl oz) single (pure) cream, whipped
6 Iced VoVo biscuits, diagonally sliced

1. Cut the jam roll into 2.5 cm (1 inch) thick slices and arrange them around the side of the trifle bowl on top of the raspberry marshmallow layer.

2. Spoon the yoghurt into the centre of the trifle, inside the border created by the jam roll slices.

3. Cover the top of the trifle with large dollops of the whipped cream.

4. Arrange the jelly cubes, raspberry marshmallow cubes and Iced VoVo biscuits on top of the trifle.

Decorating Tip

- You can purchase a jam sponge roll or make your own sponge roll following the Lemon Swiss roll recipe on page 141, replacing the lemon curd with raspberry jam.

STORAGE

- This trifle is best served chilled and eaten on the day of decorating. It can be refrigerated for up to 5 days, but the Iced VoVo biscuits and jam sponge roll will soften.

- The jelly and marshmallow layers, jelly cubes and marshmallow cubes can be prepared up to 2 days in advance and stored in the refrigerator. Cover the trifle bowl, and store the jelly cubes and marshmallow cubes in airtight containers.

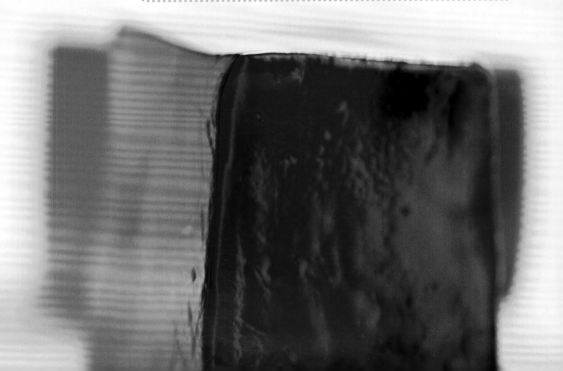

GOLDEN SYRUP STACK

When I was littler, Sunday morning blueberry pancakes slathered with butter and topped with lashings of golden syrup was the treat I looked forward to all week. I might have already mentioned that I love baking things that look like other things, so I couldn't resist the temptation of the pan-CAKE. This golden syrup stack is simply screaming for you and your friends to stick a fork in it.

SERVES 18—20

LEMON, BLUEBERRY AND BUTTERMILK CAKE

Cooking oil spray

230 g (8 oz) unsalted butter, softened

1½ cups (340 g) granulated sugar

4 eggs, at room temperature

1 tablespoon vanilla extract

2 cups (320 g) self-raising flour, sifted, plus 1 tablespoon extra

½ teaspoon salt

1 cup (250 ml) buttermilk, at room temperature

Grated zest and juice of 2 lemons

1½ cups (210 g) fresh or unthawed frozen blueberries

1. Preheat the oven to 160°C (320°F). Spray three 15 cm (6 inch) round cake tins with cooking oil spray and line with baking paper.

2. Using an electric mixer fitted with the paddle attachment, beat the butter on high speed until creamy. Add the sugar and beat on medium–high speed until light and creamy. Beat in the eggs and vanilla on medium speed until completely combined, scraping the side of the bowl as needed.

3. Slowly add the 2 cups of sifted flour and the salt. Beat on low speed for 5 seconds, then add the buttermilk, lemon zest and lemon juice. Lightly stir with a wooden spoon until everything is just combined.

4. Toss the blueberries with the extra flour and fold into the batter (the batter will be extremely thick), being careful not to over-mix.

5. Divide the batter evenly among the cake tins. Bake for 20–30 minutes or until a skewer inserted into the centre of the cakes comes out clean. Leave in the tins to cool completely before turning out.

LEMON CREAM CHEESE FROSTING

750 g (1 lb 10 oz) cream cheese, softened

⅓ cup (80 g) unsalted butter, softened

200 g (7 oz) icing (confectioners') sugar, sifted

2 tablespoons lemon juice

1. Using an electric mixer, beat the cream cheese and butter until fluffy.

2. Gradually add the icing sugar while beating. Add the lemon juice and beat until fluffy.

ASSEMBLY AND DECORATION

30 g (1 oz) chilled cream cheese
½ cup (175 g) thick golden syrup
1 handful fresh blueberries

1. Use a long, thin knife to divide each cake into two even layers.

2. Working on a cake turntable or lazy Susan, secure the bottom layer of cake onto a cake stand or board with a dollop of cream cheese frosting and then gently twist in place. Use an offset spatula to cover the top of the cake with a 1 cm (½ inch) layer of frosting, spreading it right to the edge.

3. Place the second cake layer on top and repeat the layering process until the last cake layer is added.

4. Using an offset spatula and a cake scraper, gently crumb coat the entire cake with a thin layer of frosting (see page 240). Carefully smooth the side until the desired finish is achieved. Use the offset spatula to smooth the top of the cake by gently pulling inwards from the edge of the cake into the centre, cleaning the excess frosting off the spatula with each scrape. Chill in the refrigerator for 20 minutes.

5. Slice the cream cheese to look like chunks of butter. Decorate the cake with a generous drizzle of golden syrup, the 'butter' chunks and a scattering of fresh blueberries.

THE CUTEST KOALA CAKE

Did you know that although koalas sleep for up to 19 hours of every 24, and eat over one kilogram of eucalyptus leaves a day, they can run as fast as a rabbit when they want to? The koala is truly the gold medalist of the Effortless Olympics. This magnificent marsupial is unique to our continent but has become a cuddly celebrity worldwide. Among its many quirky and adorable traits, when a koala is born it's about the size of a jellybean — tiny yet mighty!

SERVES 18—20

HONEY CINNAMON CAKE

Cooking oil spray
270 g (9½ oz) unsalted butter, softened
¾ cup (165 g) caster sugar
½ cup (160 g) honey
1½ teaspoons vanilla extract
4 large eggs, at room temperature
3 cups (480 g) self-raising flour
3 teaspoons ground cinnamon
280 ml (9¾ fl oz) milk, at room temperature

1. Preheat the oven to 160°C (320°F) fan forced. Grease two 15 cm (6 inch) round cake tins with cooking oil spray and line with baking paper.
2. Using an electric mixer, beat the butter, sugar, honey and vanilla until pale and creamy. Add the eggs, one at a time, beating well after each addition.
3. Sift the flour and cinnamon together. Fold into the butter mixture in two batches, alternating with the milk.
4. Divide the batter between the cake tins and smooth the surface. Bake for 30—40 minutes or until a skewer inserted into the centre of the cakes comes out clean. Leave to cool in the tins for 15 minutes, then carefully turn out onto a wire rack to cool completely.
5. Use a long, thin knife to divide each cake into three even layers. Cover and set aside until needed.

VANILLA BEAN SWISS MERINGUE BUTTERCREAM

1½ cups (330 g) caster sugar
8 large egg whites
2 cups (500 g) unsalted butter, softened
1 teaspoon vanilla bean paste
Pink and blue gel food colouring

1. Put the sugar and egg whites in a heatproof glass bowl. Set the bowl over a pan of gently simmering water and whisk until the sugar has dissolved and the mixture is slightly warm to the touch. Remove from the heat.
2. Using an electric mixer fitted with the whisk attachment, beat on high speed until the mixture has formed stiff and glossy peaks (about 10—15 minutes).
3. Add the butter in three batches, beating until incorporated after each addition. Add the vanilla and beat until fluffy. Tint ½ cup of the buttercream pink and the remaining buttercream blue. Cover and set aside in a cool place.

ASSEMBLY AND DECORATION

½ cup (160 g) warmed honey,
  apricot jam or golden syrup
2 large round chocolate-coated
  biscuits
4 toothpicks
50 g (1¾ oz) white fondant
Cornflour, for rolling
1 Iced VoVo biscuit (see tips)
2 small round chocolate-coated
  biscuits
30 g (1 oz) black fondant or black
  liquorice rope

1. Working on a cake turntable or lazy Susan, secure the bottom layer of cake onto a cake board or plate with a dollop of blue buttercream underneath and then gently twist in place. Use an offset spatula to spread a thin layer of honey, jam or golden syrup over the top of the cake. Cover the top of the cake with a 5 mm (¼ inch) layer of blue buttercream, then use the spatula and a cake scraper to gently crumb coat the side of the cake with a thin layer of buttercream (see page 240).

2. Place the second cake layer on top and repeat the layering process until the final layer has been crumb coated. Trim the top of the cake to create a rounded appearance, as shown. Apply another layer of buttercream to the exposed areas of cake and carefully smooth the cake until the desired finish is reached. Chill in the refrigerator for 20 minutes.

3. Apply a final layer of blue buttercream all over the chilled cake and smooth with a small cake scraper (see page 241).

4. Slice the edge of each of the chocolate-coated biscuits and insert the toothpicks. Spread or pipe some pink buttercream over the front of each biscuit. Insert the biscuits into the cake to create the koala's ears.

5. Spoon the remaining blue buttercream into a piping bag fitted with a grass tip or multi-opening tip to pipe 'fur' around the ears and on top of the head.

6. Roll out the white fondant on a board dusted with cornflour. Use a small, sharp knife to cut it to size, reserving the offcuts, then press it onto the koala's chest.

7. Stick the Iced VoVo biscuit to the koala's chest using a little buttercream. Add the small chocolate-coated biscuits in front of the chest so that the Iced VoVo is sitting between them. Pipe buttercream 'fur' over the paws.

8. Shape the black fondant or cut the liquorice to form the koala's eyes, nose and mouth details. Use a small amount of white fondant to create the whites of the koala's eyes and stick them in place using a little water, if needed. Attach the eyes, nose and mouth to the cake using a little buttercream.

Decorating Tips

- You can also bake the cakes in six 15 cm (6 inch) cake layer tins. This saves the job of cutting the cakes into layers. You'll need to reduce the cooking time to 20–30 minutes.
- I used Wagon Wheels biscuits for the koala's ears and an Iced VoVo biscuit for the koala to hold. You could also use a Mint Slice, Tim Tam or Honey Jumbles biscuit.

Layer the cakes, brushing each layer with honey, jam or golden syrup and applying a layer of buttercream.

Once you add the final cake layer, trim the top of the cake to create a slightly rounded appearance.

Apply a final layer of buttercream all over the cake and use a small cake scraper to give a smooth finish.

A grass piping tip or multi-opening piping tip is used to create the 'fur' details on the koala.

SLICE OF CHOC-MINT HEAVEN

Mint and chocolate is a powerhouse pairing to rival cheese and biscuits, fish and chips, avocado and jam (what do you mean, that's just me?). Although at times polarising (I know friendships that have ended over this), when the balance is correct, the richness of dark chocolate carrying the sweet, fragrant notes of mint is a match made in cake heaven. Of course, no one likes baked goods that taste like toothpaste (apologies if you do), so keep in mind that a little peppermint essence goes a long way.

SERVES 16

CHOC-HEAVEN CAKE

Cooking oil spray

2 cups (320 g) self-raising flour

1¾ cups (385 g) caster sugar

¾ cup (85 g) cocoa powder

1 teaspoon bicarbonate of soda (baking soda)

½ teaspoon salt

1 teaspoon instant coffee powder

1 cup (250 ml) buttermilk, at room temperature

½ cup (115 g) melted coconut oil

2 large eggs, at room temperature

2 teaspoons vanilla extract

1 cup (250 ml) boiling water

1. Preheat the oven to 160°C (320°F) fan forced. Grease two 18 cm (7 inch) round cake tins with cooking oil spray and line with baking paper.

2. Using an electric mixer fitted with the paddle attachment, whisk the flour, sugar, cocoa, bicarbonate of soda, salt and coffee powder until combined.

3. Add the buttermilk, coconut oil, eggs and vanilla and mix on medium speed until well combined. Reduce the speed, carefully add the boiling water and mix until well combined.

4. Divide the batter between the cake tins. Bake for 45–50 minutes or until a skewer inserted into the centre of the cakes comes out clean. Remove from the oven and allow the cakes to cool for about 20 minutes, then remove from the tins and transfer to a wire rack to cool completely.

MINT BUTTERCREAM

½ cup (125 g) unsalted butter, softened

1½ cups (210 g) icing (confectioners') sugar, sifted

Green gel food colouring

2 teaspoons peppermint essence

1. Using an electric mixer, beat the butter until pale and creamy.

2. Add the icing sugar, one large spoonful at a time, beating constantly until smooth and combined. Tint with the green colouring until the desired shade is reached.

3. Add a small amount of the peppermint essence and beat until combined. Continue adding the peppermint essence until you're happy with the taste.

CHOCOLATE GLAZE

7 (11 g/¼ oz) gelatine sheets
1 cup (220 g) caster sugar
⅔ cup (75 g) cocoa powder
100 ml (3½ fl oz) thick (double)
   cream
½ cup (125 ml) water
50 g (1¾ oz) dark chocolate,
   roughly chopped

1. Put the gelatine in a shallow bowl of cold water to soften for 5 minutes.

2. Combine the sugar, cocoa, cream and water in a saucepan over medium heat. Stir until melted, then bring to the boil, stirring until smooth. Remove from the heat, add the chocolate and stir until melted. Set aside to cool for 5 minutes.

3. Squeeze any liquid from the gelatine sheets and stir into the chocolate mixture until dissolved. Pour through a sieve into a bowl. Transfer the glaze to the fridge to cool and thicken for about 1 hour or until it reaches the consistency of thick mayonnaise.

ASSEMBLY AND DECORATION

2 tablespoons apricot jam, sieved
2 gummy spearmint leaves

STORAGE

- The cake is best served at room temperature. It can be refrigerated for 5 days or frozen for 2 months.
- The glaze can be made up to 3 days in advance and stored in the fridge, covered with plastic wrap. Gently reheat it and allow it to cool slightly before pouring onto the cake.

1. Working on a cake turntable or lazy Susan, use an offset spatula to cover the top of the bottom layer of cake with a generous amount of buttercream, spreading it right to the edge.

2. Place the second layer of cake on top and gently press down to secure. Use an offset spatula to smooth the excess buttercream so that it very lightly covers the side and gives a smooth edge.

3. Gently warm the apricot jam and lightly brush it over the cake, covering the side and top. Chill in the refrigerator for 30 minutes.

4. Place the chocolate glaze in a heatproof bowl and gently stir over a pan of simmering water (or microwave at 20-second intervals, stirring after each) until melted. Allow to cool slightly for 5–10 minutes.

5. Transfer the chilled cake to a wire rack sitting on a large baking tray to catch any excess glaze. Pour the glaze over the cake, making sure it completely covers the cake. Use an offset spatula to carefully smooth over the top and side, if needed.

6. Leave the cake to set for an hour or so, then carefully transfer to a cake stand or cake board. Decorate the cake with gummy spearmint leaves.

Decorating Tip

- I use a large barbecue spatula and a large offset spatula to transfer the finished cake to the cake stand, board or platter.

SYDNEY OPERA HOUSE PAV

The Sydney Opera House, with its distinctive white sails, is one of the 20th century's most famous buildings. Designed by Danish architect Jørn Utzon, it opened in 1973 and is among the most popular visitor attractions in Australia. In 2007 the Sydney Opera House was named a UNESCO World Heritage Site. In this dessert, I've combined the iconic silhouette of the Opera House sails (don't they look smashing in pink?) with our beloved pavlova, which at times can be a structural feat in its own right. So, a bit of architectural elegance meets edible engineering.

SERVES 18—20

PAVLOVA

6 egg whites
1½ cups (330 g) caster sugar
3 teaspoons cornflour
1 teaspoon white vinegar

1. Preheat the oven to 160°C (320°F) fan forced. Line a large baking tray with baking paper and draw a 20 cm (8 inch) circle on the paper.
2. Using an electric mixer, whisk the egg whites and sugar on high speed for 15 minutes or until thick and glossy and the sugar has dissolved. Whisk in the cornflour and vinegar until combined.
3. Spoon the meringue mixture onto the tray in the centre of the circle and smooth the surface. Using an offset spatula, drag the meringue upwards from the bottom into peaks.
4. Place in the oven and reduce the temperature to 100°C (200°F). Bake for 1 hour 20 minutes or until the outside of the pavlova is crisp and dry. Turn off the oven and leave the pavlova to cool in the oven with the door ajar for at least 6 hours or until cooled completely, preferably overnight.

SPICED PEACHES

½ cup (125 ml) water
⅓ cup (75 g) caster sugar
¼ teaspoon ground allspice
4 cardamom pods
1 cinnamon stick
4 peaches, stones removed, thinly sliced

1. Combine the water, sugar, allspice, cardamom pods and cinnamon stick in a saucepan. Stir over medium–low heat until the sugar has dissolved, then simmer for 8–10 minutes or until slightly thickened.
2. Place the peach slices in a heatproof bowl and pour in the syrup. Chill in the refrigerator for 1 hour.

RASPBERRY SWIRL WHITE CHOCOLATE

500 g (1 lb 2 oz) good-quality white chocolate, chopped (see tips)
Pink oil-based or powdered chocolate colouring
½ cup (20 g) freeze-dried raspberries

1. Line a large baking tray with baking paper.
2. Melt the white chocolate using either the microwave or double-boiler method (see page 245).
3. Place ⅓ cup of the melted chocolate in a smaller heatproof bowl and mix in a small amount of pink colouring until the desired shade is reached.
4. Pour the white chocolate onto the baking tray. Use an offset metal spatula or a metal spoon to spread the chocolate in an even layer over the tray.
5. Dollop the pink chocolate onto the white chocolate in various places. Working quickly, use a skewer to swirl the chocolate to create a marbled pattern. As soon as you are happy with the pattern, press the freeze-dried raspberries into the chocolate. Give the tray a little shake to help embed the raspberries. Place in the freezer for 1 hour or until completely set.
6. Carefully snap the set chocolate into sail-like shapes. If the chocolate has set firm enough, it should snap quite easily.

ASSEMBLY AND DECORATION

500 g (1 lb 2 oz) mascarpone cheese
2 teaspoons vanilla bean paste
300 ml (10½ fl oz) single (pure) cream, whipped
1 handful fresh raspberries

1. Carefully place the pavlova on a cake stand or serving plate.
2. Combine the mascarpone and vanilla in a bowl, then gently spoon into the centre of the pavlova.
3. Top the pavlova with the whipped cream and the drained peaches. Adorn with the chocolate 'sails' to emulate the sails of the Sydney Opera House. Add a handful of fresh raspberries. Serve immediately.

STORAGE

The pavlova is best served as soon as it is decorated. It can be refrigerated for 4 days, but will soften once it absorbs the moisture from the peaches.

Decorating Tips

- If you are using any type of couverture chocolate (my personal favourite), which has a high cocoa butter content, you will need to temper (also known as 'crystallise') the chocolate in order to obtain the best taste, texture and overall results. See page 245 for tips on working with chocolate.
- You will find freeze-dried raspberries in most health food stores and specialty grocers, or you can buy them online.
- You could also top the pavlova with some fresh passionfruit pulp.

Spoon the thick and glossy meringue onto the baking tray in the centre of the circle.

Use a large offset spatula to drag the meringue upwards from the bottom to form peaks.

Pour the melted white chocolate onto the tray and use an offset spatula to spread it in an even layer.

Dollop blobs of the pink chocolate onto the white chocolate all over the tray.

Working quickly, use a skewer to swirl the pink chocolate through the white chocolate to create a marbled pattern.

Gently press the freeze-dried raspberries into the melted chocolate before it sets, then gently shake the tray to help embed them.

THE ANTI-VALENTINE CAKE

Your average Aussie is a fairly shrewd beastie — no one pulls the emotional wool over our eyes. We can see through Valentine's Day with its over-commercialised, manipulative drivel (yes, we can — especially those miserable years when we don't get any cards or messages and our eyes are red from choking back the tears). So, forget the roses and sappy verses: THIS is the cake that could speak for a nation. Fill your not-in-love hearts with some realistic, fair dinkum sentiment: 'Nah mate', 'Can u not' and 'Crikey' should get you through the day in anti-romantic style.

SERVES 10—12

RED VELVET CAKE

⅔ cup (160 g) unsalted butter, softened
1½ cups (330 g) caster sugar
2 teaspoons vanilla extract
2 eggs, at room temperature
1½ cups (240 g) plain flour
1 tablespoon cocoa powder
1 cup (250 ml) buttermilk, at room temperature
2 tablespoons red food colouring

1. Preheat the oven to 160°C (320°F) fan forced. Grease three 15 cm (6 inch) round cake layer tins and line with baking paper.
2. Using an electric mixer, beat the butter, sugar and vanilla until light and fluffy. Add the eggs, one at a time, beating until just combined.
3. Stir in the flour and cocoa until just combined. Pour in the combined buttermilk and red food colouring and mix until combined, being careful not to over-mix.
4. Divide the batter among the cake tins. Bake for 30 minutes or until a skewer inserted into the centre of the cakes comes out clean. Leave the cakes to cool in the tins for at least 10 minutes before transferring to a wire rack to cool completely.

BLACK CHOCOLATE GANACHE

600 g (1 lb 5 oz) good-quality dark chocolate, chopped
300 ml (10½ fl oz) single (pure) cream
Black gel or powdered food colouring (optional)

1. Place the chocolate in a large heatproof bowl. Pour the cream into a small saucepan and heat until bubbles start to appear on the surface.
2. Pour the cream over the chocolate and stir until the chocolate has melted. Tint with a small amount of black food colouring, if using. Keep in mind that the ganache will appear one to two shades richer once set.
3. Set the ganache aside overnight at room temperature to thicken.

CONVERSATION HEARTS

200 g (7 oz) white fondant
Assorted gel food colourings
Cornflour, for rolling
Red food colouring pen
50 g (1¾ oz) white chocolate,
   melted
1 ice cream stick

1. Divide the white fondant into balls, using one for each of your chosen colours. Cover each ball with plastic wrap when it's not being used. One at a time, colour each ball of fondant and roll it out on a board dusted with cornflour. Using heart-shaped cookie cutters in different sizes, cut the coloured fondant into hearts and set aside to dry.

2. Once the hearts are dry, use the food colouring pen to decorate them. Set aside in an airtight container until needed.

3. To make the large heart cake topper, apply melted white chocolate to the centre of one of the large fondant hearts and place the ice cream stick on top. Add a little more melted chocolate, then press a second large heart on top and set aside to dry completely.

ASSEMBLY AND DECORATION

STORAGE

- The cake is best eaten at room temperature. It can be stored in the refrigerator for up to 1 week. Fondant can soften once chilled, so it's best to add the fondant hearts just before serving.

- The fondant hearts can be made up to 1 month in advance. Store them in an airtight container in a cool, dry and dark environment.

1. Working on a cake turntable or lazy Susan, secure the bottom layer of cake onto a cake stand or board with a dollop of ganache and then gently twist in place. Use an offset spatula to cover the top of the cake with a 1 cm (½ inch) layer of ganache, spreading it right to the edge. If the ganache appears too thick, gently reheat it to a more workable consistency.

2. Place the second cake layer on top and top it with another layer of the ganache. Place the third cake on top and press down to secure.

3. Using an offset spatula and a cake scraper, gently crumb coat the entire cake with a thin layer of ganache, reheating the ganache if needed (see page 240). Carefully smooth the side until the desired finish is achieved. Chill in the refrigerator for 20 minutes.

4. Apply another layer of the ganache to the chilled cake and use the cake scraper and offset spatula to smooth the side and top (see page 241) — or you may choose a more rustic finish.

5. Decorate the cake with the fondant conversation hearts, using a little water or left-over ganache to stick them to the cake, if needed.

Decorating Tips

- I used pink, lavender, blue, yellow and apricot gel food colourings.
- You can prepare the ganache using the microwave. Combine the chocolate and cream in a microwave-safe bowl and microwave on High in 1-minute intervals, stirring for 2 minutes in between, until there are no lumps. I use a stick blender to stir the cream and melted chocolate together as it's much quicker and easier to ensure an even consistency.

Working with one ball of fondant at a time, roll the fondant out on a board dusted with cornflour.

Use a set of heart-shaped cookie cutters in various sizes to make the coloured fondant hearts.

Carefully remove the excess fondant from around the hearts and leave them to dry.

Use a red food colouring pen to draw an outline around the fondant hearts and add the messages.

To make the heart cake topper, use some melted white chocolate to sandwich an ice cream stick between two of the large hearts.

Once you have added the final layer of ganache to the cake, add the fondant conversation hearts.

AUSTRALIAN CHRISTMAS TRIFLE

Dessert is no trifling matter. For the uninitiated, a trifle is a traditional English pudding made with layers of fruit, sponge soaked in alcohol, custard, sometimes jelly, and whipped cream. Nowadays, the contents of a trifle can be variable, making this the perfect dessert to house all of your favourite bits and bobs! Serve this at Christmas, as a lighter version of the traditional dense Christmas pudding. My favourite Australian recipe includes the fragrant summery flavours of lemon myrtle, coconut and vanilla custard, with lots of satisfying lusciousness and crunch.

SERVES 20

LEMON SWISS ROLL

3 eggs, at room temperature, separated
½ cup (110 g) caster sugar, plus 2 tablespoons for rolling
¾ cup (120 g) self-raising flour, sifted
2 tablespoons hot milk
¼ cup (75 g) lemon curd (page 246 or store-bought), warmed
1 teaspoon freshly ground lemon myrtle (see tips)

1. Preheat the oven to 180°C (350°F) fan forced. Grease a 26 x 32 cm (10½ x 12½ inch) Swiss roll tin and line with baking paper.

2. Using an electric mixer, beat the egg whites in a small bowl until soft peaks form. Gradually add the sugar, beating until dissolved after each addition.

3. Add the egg yolks, one at a time, beating well until thick and light. Fold in the flour and hot milk.

4. Gently spread the batter into the tin. Bake for 10–15 minutes or until the top is golden.

5. Meanwhile, lightly sprinkle a sheet of baking paper with the extra sugar. Turn the hot sponge out onto the paper and carefully peel away the lining paper. Allow to cool for 5–10 minutes, then trim the sides of the sponge.

6. Roll up the sponge from the short side, then unroll. Spread evenly with the lemon curd and sprinkle with the lemon myrtle. Re-roll from the same short side by lifting the paper and using it as a guide. Cover with plastic wrap or store in an airtight container until needed.

COCONUT BISCUIT CRUMB

½ cup (80 g) plain flour
1 cup (100 g) rolled oats
¼ cup (40 g) brown sugar
¼ cup (20 g) shredded coconut
100 g (3½ oz) salted butter, chopped

1. Preheat the oven to 180°C (350°F) fan forced.

2. Combine the flour, oats, brown sugar and coconut in a bowl. Rub in the butter until the mixture resembles coarse breadcrumbs.

3. Sprinkle the crumb mixture over a baking tray. Bake for 10 minutes or until golden and crisp. Allow to cool completely before assembling the trifle.

ASSEMBLY AND DECORATION

300 ml (10½ fl oz) single (pure) cream

1 teaspoon freshly ground lemon myrtle (see tips)

2 cups (500 ml) thick vanilla custard

1 cup (300 g) lemon curd (page 246 or store-bought)

1 cup (260 g) plain coconut yoghurt or thick Greek-style yoghurt

6 egg whites

¾ cup (165 g) caster sugar

Grated lime zest, for sprinkling

Edible gold leaf flakes

1. Whip the cream with the lemon myrtle until soft peaks form.

2. Spoon the coconut biscuit crumb mixture into a large trifle bowl and top with the custard. Cover with a layer of lemon curd and top with half of the whipped cream.

3. Cut the lemon Swiss roll into 2.5 cm (1 inch) thick slices and arrange them around the side of the trifle bowl on top of the cream.

4. Spoon the yoghurt into the centre of the trifle, inside the border created by the Swiss roll slices. Smooth the surface with a spatula. Top with the remaining whipped cream and smooth the surface with the clean spatula.

5. Put the egg whites and sugar in a heatproof glass bowl. Set the bowl over a pan of gently simmering water and whisk constantly for 8–10 minutes or until the mixture is frothy, the sugar has dissolved and the temperature reaches 72°C (160°F) on a candy thermometer.

6. Transfer the mixture to the bowl of an electric mixer. Using the whisk attachment, whip on medium speed for 5–8 minutes or until the mixture holds stiff and glossy peaks.

7. Spoon the meringue into a piping bag fitted with a 2 cm (¾ inch) round or star nozzle and pipe 'kisses' all over the top of the trifle. Use a small kitchen blowtorch to gently brown the meringue. Sprinkle with the lime zest and gold leaf flakes. Enjoy with your nearest and dearest!

STORAGE

- This trifle is best served chilled and eaten on the day of decorating. It can be refrigerated for up to 5 days, but the Swiss roll may soften and the meringue may deflate.

- The meringue topping can be piped onto the trifle and browned with the blowtorch a few hours before serving.

Decorating Tips

- It's fine to use store-bought custard – make sure it's nice and thick!
- You can also use pasteurised egg whites from a carton to make the meringue. You won't need to whisk the sugar into the egg whites over a pan of simmering water – simply place the sugar and egg whites directly into the mixer.
- If you don't have a kitchen blowtorch, place the trifle under a hot grill for 30 seconds or until the meringue is lightly browned.
- Look for lemon myrtle in specialty ingredient stores, farmers' markets or online. You can replace it with the same quantity of grated lemon zest.

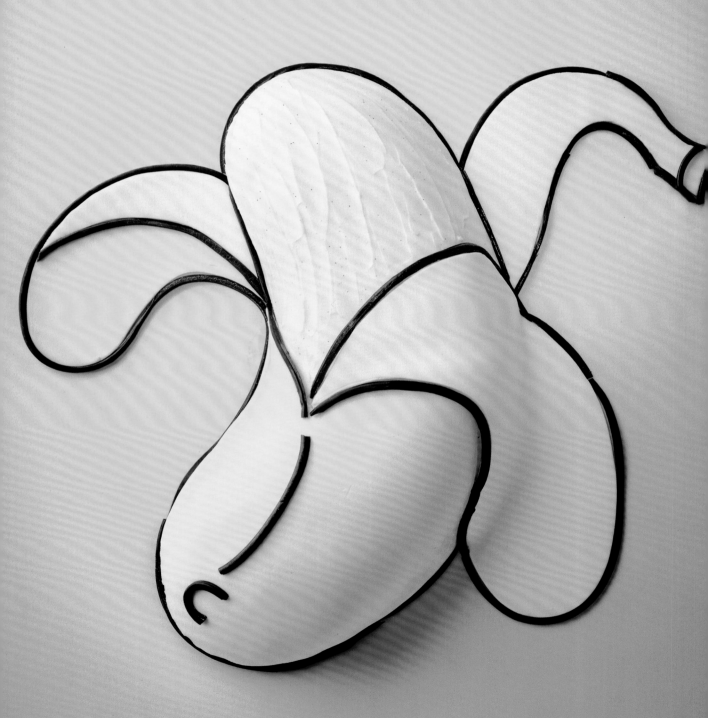

THE BIG BANANA

This book wouldn't be complete without my version of Australia's original and most famous 'Big Thing'. Our beloved Big Banana was built in the city of Coffs Harbour in 1964 and is now home to its own amusement park. (Weird? Who are you calling weird?) The Big Banana has proved so popular over the decades that it even had a postage stamp printed in its honour. This recipe uses my favourite banana cake and home-made marshmallow fondant (I always find home-made much more a-PEEL-ing). Your little monkeys will think this cake is a bunch of fun.

SERVES 16

BANANA CAKE

3⅓ cups (535 g) self-raising flour
2 teaspoons bicarbonate of soda (baking soda)
½ teaspoon salt
1 cup (250 ml) olive oil
2 cups (320 g) brown sugar
⅓ cup (110 g) honey
2 tablespoons ground cinnamon
1 tablespoon vanilla extract
4 large eggs
6 large ripe bananas, about 800 g (1 lb 12 oz), mashed
⅓ cup (90 g) plain yoghurt
3 cups (330 g) walnuts, chopped

Preheat the oven to 150°C (300°F) fan forced. Grease a 30 cm (12 inch) square baking tin and line the base with baking paper.

Put the flour, bicarbonate of soda and salt in a bowl and mix to combine.

Whisk the olive oil and brown sugar in a large bowl, breaking up any lumps. Add the honey, cinnamon and vanilla, whisking until smooth. Add the eggs, one at a time, and beat until fully incorporated, then stir in the banana, yoghurt and walnuts. Gently fold in the flour mixture until combined.

Pour the batter into the tin. Bake for 1½ hours or until a skewer inserted into the centre of the cake comes out clean. Leave to cool in the tin. Cover the cake and tin with plastic wrap, then place in the fridge to set firm.

VANILLA CREAM CHEESE FROSTING

1.2 kg (2 lb 11 oz) cream cheese, softened
100 g (3½ oz) unsalted butter, softened
2 teaspoons vanilla bean paste
300 g (10½ oz) icing (confectioners') sugar, sifted
2 tablespoons lemon juice

Using an electric mixer, beat the cream cheese, butter and vanilla until fluffy.

Gradually add the icing sugar while beating. Add the lemon juice and beat until fluffy.

ASSEMBLY AND DECORATION

Icing (confectioners') sugar or
cornflour, for rolling
1 quantity yellow marshmallow
fondant (page 247)
1 quantity white marshmallow
fondant (page 247)
Piping gel or edible sugar glue
Black liquorice rope

STORAGE

This cake is best served at room temperature. It can be refrigerated for up to 5 days.

Carefully turn the chilled banana cake out onto a large chopping board or clean bench. Using a sharp knife, carefully cut out a large banana shape, working on the diagonal. Trim to create the curved sides. (Remember to save the cake offcuts to avoid waste – see tips, below.)

Secure the cake onto a cake board or serving tray with a dollop of cream cheese frosting and then gently twist in place. Using an offset spatula and a cake scraper, gently crumb coat the entire cake with a thin layer of cream cheese frosting (see page 240). Carefully smooth the top and side until the desired finish is achieved. Chill in the refrigerator for 15–20 minutes.

Apply a generous layer of cream cheese frosting to the chilled cake and use the cake scraper and offset spatula to smooth the side and top (see page 241) – or you may choose a more rustic finish. Wipe any excess frosting off the board using a clean damp cloth. Return the cake to the refrigerator for another 30 minutes or until firm.

Dust a clean surface with sifted icing sugar or cornflour and roll out the yellow fondant. Carefully drape the fondant over the bottom half of the chilled cake. Use a small, sharp knife or scalpel to trim it to fit the cake, leaving some excess for the open peel.

Re-roll the remaining yellow fondant and roll out the white fondant. Carefully drape the white fondant over the yellow fondant and re-roll so that the layers 'fuse' together. Use a small, sharp knife or scalpel to cut out three banana peel shapes. Using the picture as a guide, arrange the banana peels in place over and around the cake.

Use a thin brush and piping gel or edible sugar glue to add detail to the banana peel with a thin outline of sliced liquorice rope.

Decorating Tips

Don't throw away the cake offcuts! Either serve warm, topped with ice cream (yuuuuum!), or store in an airtight container in the freezer for up to 2 months... or until needed for an 'emergency' dessert.

For a nut-free cake, omit the walnuts from the banana cake.

THE BONDI HIPSTER (RAW VEGAN) CAKE

Bought a scoby off the internet so you can make organic kombucha? Writing your first poetry collection on a vintage typewriter? Only ever watch foreign films? You're possibly a hipster. And if you live near my fave beach, you're a Bondi hipster. This raw, vegan, gluten-free and refined-sugar-free cake is my present to you. You'll need a semi-sphere silicone mould for this recipe. (Special equipment for the hipster cake? Who would've thought?) I used a mould with 24 cavities, each with a diameter of 3.5 cm (1½ inches). Enjoy with a glass of that kombucha.

SERVES 14

FILLING

3 cups (450 g) raw cashews
2 cups (500 ml) coconut milk
1 cup (340 g) rice malt syrup
½ cup (115 g) coconut oil
⅓ cup (80 ml) lemon or lime juice
**¼ cup (60 g) sunflower lecithin
    or GMO-free soy lecithin**
1¼ tablespoons chia seeds
**1 vanilla bean or 2 teaspoons vanilla
    bean paste**
1 teaspoon matcha green tea powder
**Natural food colouring gels in green,
    yellow, pink and purple (optional)**
1 greased 24-hole semi-sphere mould
½ teaspoon turmeric powder
½ cup (75 g) frozen raspberries
½ cup (75 g) frozen blueberries

BASE

1 cup (150 g) macadamia nuts
½ cup (70 g) pistachio nuts
½ cup (90 g) raw buckwheat
8–9 pitted medjool dates
1 teaspoon ground cinnamon
½ teaspoon sea salt

1. Combine the cashews and coconut milk for the filling in a large bowl. Leave to soak overnight.

2. To make the base, grease an 18 cm (7 inch) round spring-form cake tin and line the base with baking paper. Combine the macadamia nuts, pistachio nuts, buckwheat, pitted dates, cinnamon and sea salt in a food processor and whiz until the mixture is the size of breadcrumbs and begins to stick together. Press the mixture firmly into the base of the cake tin. Place in the freezer while you prepare the filling.

3. For the filling, tip the cashews and coconut milk into the food processor bowl and add the rice malt syrup, coconut oil, lemon or lime juice, lecithin, chia seeds and seeds scraped from the split vanilla bean or vanilla bean paste and blend until smooth.

4. Divide the cashew mixture into four portions, leaving one portion in the food processor bowl and dividing the other three portions among three separate bowls.

5. Colour the first bowl of filling with the matcha powder and green colouring, if using. Use a spoon to fill six cavities of the greased semi-sphere mould and gently tap to level. Pour the remaining matcha mixture on top of the base. Place the mould and cake tin in the freezer for at least 30 minutes or until the filling is firm.

6. Colour the second bowl of filling with the turmeric powder and yellow colouring, if using. Fill another six cavities of the mould and gently tap to level. Pour the remaining turmeric mixture on top of the matcha layer. Return the mould and cake tin to the freezer for at least 30 minutes or until the filling is firm.

7. Put the raspberries in the food processor containing the reserved filling and blend until smooth. Add the pink colouring, if using. Fill another six cavities of the mould and gently tap to level. Pour the remaining raspberry mixture on top of the turmeric layer. Return the mould and cake tin to the freezer for at least 30 minutes or until the filling is firm.

8. Put the blueberries and the remaining filling in the cleaned food processor and blend until smooth. Add the purple colouring, if using. Fill the final six cavities of the mould and gently tap to level. Pour the remaining blueberry mixture on top of the raspberry layer. Return the mould and cake tin to the freezer for at least 2 hours or until frozen.

9. Release the frozen cake from the spring-form tin, running a small, sharp knife around the inside of the tin, if needed. Transfer the cake to a cake stand or serving plate and place in the refrigerator to thaw for at least 2 hours before serving.

DECORATION

1 handful fresh raspberries
1 handful fresh blueberries
Organic edible flowers

1. Decorate the top of the cake with the mousse semi-spheres, raspberries, blueberries and edible flowers. Cut the cake into slices and serve with additional mousse semi-spheres.

STORAGE

This cake is best enjoyed straight from the fridge. It can be refrigerated for up to 4 days.

Decorating Tips

- You can replace the rice malt syrup with honey or coconut nectar, to taste.
- The food colouring is optional, but will add a richer shade to each layer.
- Any left-over mousse semi-spheres can be frozen for up to a month.

MARVELLOUS MILO® FUDGE CAKE

Milo was created in 1934 by Aussie Thomas Mayne, who launched it at the Sydney Royal Easter Show. He named his drink after an Olympic wrestler of ancient Greece, Milo of Croton, who was famous for carrying a bull on his shoulders. This chocolate malt powder is mixed with milk to produce a beverage that's popular around the world. But don't stop at 'beverage' – here it's melted through chocolate ganache and the malt lends a toasty, savoury richness of flavour. No bull.

SERVES 12

CHOC-HEAVEN CAKE

Cooking oil spray
1½ cups (240 g) self-raising flour
1¼ cups (275 g) caster sugar
½ cup (55 g) cocoa powder
½ teaspoon bicarbonate of soda
   (baking soda)
1 pinch salt
½ teaspoon instant coffee powder
¾ cup (185 ml) buttermilk, at room
   temperature
⅓ cup (80 g) melted coconut oil
2 large eggs, at room temperature
1 teaspoon vanilla extract
½ cup (125 ml) boiling water

1. Preheat the oven to 160°C (320°F) fan forced. Grease three 15 cm (6 inch) round cake tins with cooking oil spray and line with baking paper.

2. Using an electric mixer fitted with the paddle attachment, whisk the flour, sugar, cocoa, bicarbonate of soda, salt and coffee powder until combined.

3. Add the buttermilk, coconut oil, eggs and vanilla and mix on medium speed until well combined. Reduce the speed, carefully add the boiling water and mix until well combined.

4. Divide the batter among the cake tins. Bake for 35–40 minutes or until a skewer inserted into the centre of the cakes comes out clean. Remove from the oven and allow the cakes to cool for about 20 minutes, then remove from the tins and transfer to a wire rack to cool completely. Wrap in plastic wrap or a clean, damp tea towel and refrigerate until needed.

MILO GANACHE

400 ml (14 fl oz) single (pure) cream
800 g (1 lb 12 oz) good-quality dark
   chocolate, chopped
½ cup (70 g) Milo

1. Pour the cream into a small saucepan and bring to a rolling boil (there should be bubbles all over the surface, not just around the edge). Remove from the heat and add the chocolate, stirring until there are no lumps. Add the Milo and stir until dissolved.

2. Refrigerate the ganache until it is firm and thickened to the consistency of peanut butter.

BUTTERSCOTCH TOFFEE SHARDS

10 Werther's Original candies

1. Preheat the oven to 150°C (300°F). Line a baking tray with baking paper.
2. Place the unwrapped candies in a resealable plastic bag and crush into pieces using a rolling pin or a pestle.
3. Remove the wrappers and spread the crushed candies on the tray. Bake for 5–10 minutes or until completely melted. Remove from the oven and allow to cool completely.
4. Using a rolling pin or pestle, gently break the toffee into smaller shards. Store in an airtight container until needed.

ASSEMBLY AND DECORATION

30 Maltesers
1 Cadbury Flake bar, broken into smaller pieces
Edible gold lustre dust

STORAGE

The cake is best served at room temperature on the day of decorating. It can be refrigerated in an airtight container for up to 5 days.

1. Use a rolling pin to crush 20 of the Maltesers. Set aside.
2. Working on a cake turntable or lazy Susan, secure the bottom layer of cake onto a cake board or plate with a dollop of Milo ganache and then gently twist in place.
3. Fill a pastry bag fitted with a circular or star nozzle with Milo ganache. Starting from the outside edge, pipe the filling onto the cake layer until completely covered. Sprinkle with a third of the crushed Maltesers and Flake pieces.
4. Repeat with the remaining cake layers, ganache, crushed Maltesers and Flake pieces. If the ganache appears too soft, you may need to refrigerate both the cake layers and the ganache-filled piping bag between stacking each layer until a workable consistency is achieved.
5. Adorn the top of the cake with whole Maltesers and broken toffee shards. Add a decadent touch by sprinkling with edible gold dust.

Decorating Tips

- You can prepare the ganache using the microwave. Combine the chocolate and cream in a microwave-safe bowl and microwave on High in 1-minute intervals, stirring for 2 minutes in between, until there are no lumps. Add the Milo and stir until dissolved. I use a stick blender to stir the cream and melted chocolate together as it's much quicker and easier to ensure an even consistency.
- If you need to speed up the ganache cooling time, place it in the freezer, stirring every 15 minutes, until nice and thick.
- You could use any boiled candy to make the toffee shards.

Hold the piping bag upright as you pipe blobs of the Milo ganache all over the cake layer.

Sprinkle a third of the crushed Maltesers and crumbled Flake pieces over the piped Milo ganache.

Add the second cake layer and gently press down, then pipe another layer of Milo ganache all over the top.

Once the final layer of Milo ganache has been sprinkled with the crushed Maltesers and flake pieces, add the whole Maltesers.

HONEY ANT TART

The honey ant is another amazing Aussie critter. With their huge, golden, honey-filled bodies, these ants are fed by their worker colleagues to fatten them up in case the food runs out — so they become living larders for the rest of the colony. They've been a sweet treat and source of food for our Indigenous Australians for thousands of years. If you don't have honey ants lying around, waiting to fulfil their life's purpose by decorating this tart, then you'll need to make your own. And try not to leave this sweet pastry unattended — you might find a colony of uninvited worker ants crashing your party.

SERVES 16

PASTRY CRUST

Butter or cooking oil spray,
    for greasing
1½ cups (240 g) plain flour,
    plus extra for rolling
¼ teaspoon salt
½ cup (125 g) cold unsalted
    butter, cubed
1 large egg
2 tablespoons iced water,
    approximately

1. Preheat the oven to 190°C (375°F) fan forced. Grease a 23 cm (9 inch) loose-based tart tin with butter or cooking oil spray.

2. Add the flour, salt and butter to the bowl of a food processor. Pulse until the butter forms pea-sized pieces. Add the egg and water and pulse again until the dough just begins to form. Add a little more water, if needed. Use your hands to shape the dough into a rough disc.

3. Roll out the dough on a lightly floured surface to a circle large enough to generously line the tart tin. Carefully ease the dough into the tin and use a sharp knife to trim the dough, leaving about 2.5 cm (1 inch) excess. Fold the dough back into the tin to create a double layer of pastry around the side and press the two layers together. Refrigerate for 30 minutes.

4. Bake the pastry for 12–15 minutes or until the crust is cooked but still light in colour. Set aside to cool completely.

HONEY RICOTTA FILLING

4 large eggs
1 cup (320 g) honey
¼ cup (55 g) unsalted butter, melted
½ cup (120 g) ricotta cheese
1 cup (140 g) blanched sliced
    almonds
⅓ cup (110 g) apricot jam, warmed

1. Preheat the oven to 160°C (320°F).

2. Whisk the eggs, honey, melted butter and ricotta together in a large bowl. Stir in the almonds. Carefully pour the filling into the crust — it should come right up to the edge.

3. Bake the tart for about 30 minutes or until the filling is caramel in colour. Put the tin on a wire rack to cool completely (this will take around 4 hours).

4. Carefully unmould the tart from the tin. Brush the warm apricot jam over the top of the tart.

DECORATION

4 large chocolate balls
Edible gold dust or edible gold paint
4 chocolate-coated almonds
4 chocolate-coated sultanas or
   peanuts
Black liquorice rope
Melted chocolate, for attaching
   the decorations (see tips)

1. Brush the chocolate balls with edible gold dust or paint. Arrange the chocolate-coated almonds on the tart, followed by the chocolate-coated sultanas or peanuts and golden chocolate balls.

2. Use a sharp knife or scissors to cut the liquorice rope into ant legs, and place them around each of the ant bodies.

3. Cut tiny antennae from the liquorice rope and attach them to the ant heads using a tiny amount of melted chocolate.

Decorating Tips

- I used Lindt Lindor Balls for the ant bodies.
- I put a chocolate-coated sultana in the microwave for 10 seconds, and used the melted chocolate to attach the antennae.

STORAGE

This tart is best enjoyed on the day it's made, but can be refrigerated for up to 5 days or frozen for up to 2 months. Add the decorations just before serving.

KOOKABURRA CAKE

The distinctive 'laugh' of the larrikin kookaburra is the soundtrack to Australia, both in the Outback and in our suburban gardens. These handsome birds belong to the kingfisher family and are often found hunting for insects and other meaty treats — you'll find them watching with beady eyes at park barbecues wherever small children are wielding poorly guarded sausage sandwiches. Their beautiful feathered strokes of electric blue look like a painting. I've included a handy template (see page 163) to help you create your own edible artwork.

SERVES 20

CARROT CAKE

Cooking oil spray

½ cup (85 g) sultanas or currants

2¼ cups (360 g) self-raising flour

1 teaspoon salt

1½ teaspoons ground cinnamon

¼ teaspoon ground nutmeg

¼ teaspoon ground allspice

¼ teaspoon ground cloves

¾ cup (85 g) walnuts, coarsely chopped

4 large eggs, at room temperature

1 cup (220 g) caster sugar

½ cup (80 g) dark brown sugar

1¼ cups (310 ml) vegetable oil or melted coconut oil

450 g (1 lb) carrots, peeled and shredded (see tips)

1. Preheat the oven to 160°C (320°F) fan forced. Grease a 26 cm (10 inch) square cake tin with cooking oil spray and line the tin with baking paper.

2. Soak the sultanas or currants in a bowl of hot water for 15 minutes. Drain and set aside.

3. Whisk the flour, salt, cinnamon, nutmeg, allspice and cloves in a large bowl. Transfer ¼ cup of the mixture to a small bowl and add the walnuts and the sultanas or currants, tossing to combine.

4. Using a food processor or an electric mixer fitted with the whisk attachment, mix the eggs and sugars until blended. With the machine running, slowly add the oil in a steady stream until combined.

5. Add the egg mixture to the flour mixture and stir until well combined, then stir in the shredded carrot and the walnut mixture.

6. Pour the batter into the cake tin. Bake for about 50 minutes or until a skewer inserted into the centre of the cake comes out clean. Leave in the tin to cool completely before turning out. Cover and set aside.

VANILLA CREAM CHEESE FROSTING

400 g (14 oz) cream cheese,
  softened
150 g (5½ oz) unsalted butter,
  softened
2 teaspoons vanilla bean paste
1 pinch salt
4 cups (560 g) icing (confectioners')
  sugar, sifted
2 teaspoons lemon juice

1. Using an electric mixer fitted with the paddle attachment, mix the cream cheese, butter, vanilla and salt on low speed until combined, then increase the speed to medium–high and beat until light and fluffy, about 2 minutes.

2. Stop the mixer and add half of the icing sugar and the lemon juice. Mix on low speed to combine. Mix in the remaining icing sugar in two batches, keeping the speed on low. Once the icing sugar is incorporated, increase the speed to medium–high and beat until light and fluffy, about 1 minute.

ASSEMBLY AND DECORATION

½ cup (75 g) dried apricots
About 25 blue cloud gummies
½ cup (25 g) coconut flakes
½ cup (70 g) natural sliced almonds
3 dried bananas, sliced
1 liquorice roll
1 Cadbury Flake bar
Black liquorice rope

1. Use an offset spatula to cover the cake with cream cheese frosting. Smooth with the spatula or a cake scraper until the desired finish is reached.

2. Trace the kookaburra template opposite onto a sheet of baking paper with a non-toxic marker or pencil. Cut out the outline and place it on the cake. Use a toothpick, skewer or small knife to trace the kookaburra onto the cake.

3. Using a small, sharp knife, slice the dried apricots and blue cloud gummies into feather-like slivers.

4. Following the picture on page 160, fill in the texture of the kookaburra's feathers by adding coconut flakes, sliced almonds, blue cloud gummies and dried apricots. Use dried bananas to make the branch.

5. Add the eye using the liquorice roll and a tiny piece of the coconut, then use the Flake bar, liquorice rope and dried banana to make the beak.

STORAGE

- This cake is best served at room temperature. It can be refrigerated for up to 5 days.
- The unfrosted cake can be placed in an airtight container or wrapped in plastic wrap and refrigerated for 3–5 days. It can also be frozen for up to 1 month. Thaw the cake overnight in the fridge before frosting.

Decorating Tips

- For a richer cake, chop the carrots and blitz them in a food processor until they are the size of couscous balls.
- You can speed up the time the cake takes to cool by placing the tin in the fridge, covered with a clean tea towel.
- To prevent crumbs running through the frosting, drop large dollops of frosting onto the cake with the spatula and then gently push the frosting outwards, rather than scraping the spatula directly over the cake crust.
- For a nut-free cake, omit the walnuts from the carrot cake and replace the kookaburra's almond 'feathers' with slivers of jersey caramels or milk chocolate shavings.

KOOKABURRA CAKE

Trace the template onto
a sheet of baking paper.

MOZZIE BITE BISCUITS

Fly swatters at the ready... The quietly menacing, warning whine of the Aussie mozzie is not something anyone wants to hear as darkness falls. These marshmallowy mouthfuls of raspberry and lemon deliciousness are far more enjoyable than their annoyingly, unbearably, aggravatingly itchy namesakes, but you could find yourself swatting eager hands away from these too. Some might say they're a tad more involved than your average tea-time bikkie, but these bites are worth the fight.

MAKES 15

SUGAR COOKIES

1½ cups (240 g) plain flour, sifted
½ teaspoon salt
100 g (3½ oz) unsalted butter, softened
½ cup (110 g) caster sugar
1 egg, chilled
1 teaspoon vanilla extract or vanilla bean paste

1. Sift the flour and salt into a large bowl.
2. Using an electric mixer fitted with the paddle attachment, cream the butter and sugar until fluffy and pale. Beat in the egg.
3. Add the flour mixture and mix on low speed until thoroughly combined. Mix in the vanilla.
4. Form the dough into a ball and place on a large piece of plastic wrap. Wrap the sides of the plastic over the ball, then press down with the palm of your hand to make a disc about 2.5 cm (1 inch) thick. Finish wrapping the disc with the plastic. Chill the dough for about 30 minutes.
5. Unwrap the dough, place on a large piece of baking paper or silicone mat and roll out until 5 mm (¼ inch) thick. Slide the baking paper or mat and dough onto a board, then refrigerate for about 15 minutes.
6. Preheat the oven to 160°C (320°F) fan forced. Line two baking trays with baking paper or silicone baking mats.
7. Cut the chilled dough into shapes using a 6 cm (2½ inch) round cookie cutter. Place on the lined trays, leaving 2.5 cm (1 inch) clearance around each one. Reserve any excess dough.
8. Put the trays of cookies in the freezer for 15 minutes. Transfer the trays to the oven and bake the cookies for 12–15 minutes or until the edges are slightly golden. Leave the trays on wire racks to cool for 15 minutes, then gently remove the cookies to finish cooling.
9. Repeat the rolling, cutting and baking with the remaining cookie dough.

RASPBERRY MARSHMALLOW AND LEMON CENTRE

1 cup (300 g) lemon curd (page 246 or store-bought), chilled
250 g (9 oz) caster sugar
½ cup (125 ml) water
2 large egg whites
70 ml (2¼ fl oz) warm water
1½ tablespoons powdered gelatine
1 cup (150 g) frozen raspberries, thawed and puréed
1 teaspoon vanilla extract
Pink gel food colouring (optional)

1. Spoon the lemon curd into a small piping bag with the tip cut off at 1 cm (½ inch). Pipe a dollop of lemon curd into the centre of each sugar cookie. Place on a tray and freeze until firm.

2. Place the sugar and ½ cup of water in a large heavy-based saucepan. Bring to the boil over high heat, without stirring. Once the syrup reaches around 110°C (230°F) on a candy thermometer, use an electric mixer to whip the egg whites into firm peaks. Continue cooking the syrup.

3. Meanwhile, pour the warm water into a small bowl and add the gelatine.

4. When the syrup reaches 120°C (250°F), remove the pan from the heat and gently stir in the gelatine mixture until well combined. With the mixer on the highest speed, continue to whip the egg whites whilst carefully pouring in the hot syrup. Add the raspberry purée, vanilla and food colouring, if using. Whip until the mixture increases in volume and thickens to form stiff peaks.

5. Spoon the marshmallow into a large piping bag fitted with a 1 cm (½ inch) circular nozzle. Remove the cookie bases from the freezer and generously pipe the marshmallow over the lemon curd so that it covers the cookies completely. Refrigerate for at least 1 hour or until completely set.

ASSEMBLY AND DECORATION

300 g (10½ oz) good-quality white chocolate, chopped
1 tablespoon coconut oil
Pink oil-based chocolate colouring (optional)
15 gummy raspberries or fresh raspberries
20 g (¾ oz) freeze-dried strawberries, crushed (optional)

1. Melt the chocolate and coconut oil using either the microwave or double-boiler method (see page 245). Stir until combined. Add the colouring, if using.

2. Transfer the chocolate to a small, deep bowl and leave to cool slightly. Dip each biscuit into the chocolate, then adorn with a raspberry and sprinkle with the crushed strawberries, if using. Refrigerate until completely set.

Decorating Tip

- You will find freeze-dried strawberries in health food stores and specialty grocers, or buy them online. You can also use freeze-dried raspberries.

STORAGE

- The biscuits can be refrigerated in an airtight container for 5–7 days, or frozen for up to 2 months (the fresh raspberries will soften if frozen).
- The undecorated biscuits can be stored in an airtight container at room temperature for up to 2 weeks. They also freeze well.

THE TIM TAM™ TRIPLE

My favourite biscuit (and probably the whole of Australia's), the Tim Tam is the luxurious, smooth-talking aristocrat of the bikkie world. Introduced in 1964, the Tim Tam is best consumed while wearing cosy pyjamas and a pair of Ugg boots – extensive personal research has proved this. Being a fan of bogan-luxury myself, I love that this very decadent dessert doesn't take as much effort as you might think. The hardest part about making this no-bake cheesecake is finding the willpower to resist downing an entire packet of Tim Tams.

SERVES 16

18 Tim Tam Dark chocolate biscuits

50 g (1¾ oz) butter, melted

500 g (1 lb 2 oz) cream cheese, softened

1 cup (250 ml) single (pure) cream

250 g (9 oz) white chocolate, melted

3 Tim Tam White chocolate biscuits, chopped

250 g (9 oz) dark chocolate, melted

3 Tim Tam Original chocolate biscuits, chopped

200 ml (7 fl oz) single (pure) cream, extra, whipped

5 Tim Tam biscuits, extra, to serve

½ cup (125 ml) salted caramel, to serve (page 246 or store-bought)

1. Grease an 18 cm (7 inch) round spring-form cake tin and line the base with baking paper. Put the dark chocolate Tim Tams in a food processor and process until finely crushed. Add the melted butter and process until well combined. Spoon into the cake tin and press over the base. Refrigerate for 30 minutes or until firm.

2. Put half of the cream cheese and half of the cream into the clean food processor bowl and process until smooth. Add the melted white chocolate and process until smooth. Pour the mixture over the base and gently jiggle from side to side to smooth the surface. Stud with the chopped white chocolate Tim Tams. Refrigerate for 1 hour or until just set.

3. Put the remaining cream cheese and cream into the clean food processor bowl and process until smooth. Add the melted dark chocolate and process until smooth. Pour the mixture over the white chocolate layer. Again, gently jiggle from side to side to smooth the surface. Stud with the chopped milk chocolate Tim Tams. Refrigerate for 2 hours or until completely set.

4. Transfer the cheesecake to the freezer for 1 hour. Carefully remove the cheesecake from the tin and place on a serving platter. Set aside to thaw for 1 hour (or refrigerate until 1 hour before serving).

5. Just before serving, decorate the cheesecake with the whipped cream, chopped Tim Tams and salted caramel.

Decorating Tip

- You can speed up the setting process by placing the cheesecake in the freezer once the final layer has been added. Allow it to thaw at room temperature before decorating and serving.

STORAGE

This cake is best enjoyed on the day of decorating (straight from the fridge or at room temperature). It can be refrigerated in an airtight container for up to 5 days.

YOU BEAUT BBQ

The BBQ (pronounce it 'barbie-q', or shorten to 'barbie') is an Australian institution. It brings everyone together over the smell of sizzling sausages (better known as 'snags'), beers, banter and backyard cricket. Any excuse for a barbie is welcome here. Picnic at the beach? Aussie BBQ. Game of footy at the local park? Aussie BBQ. Backyard party? Aussie BBQ. Shopping at the hardware store? Aussie BBQ! This cake celebrates the quintessential Aussie BBQ with all of your favourite trimmings, cooked to perfection.

SERVES 16—18

CARAMEL MUDCAKE

200 g (7 oz) unsalted butter, chopped
200 g (7 oz) good-quality white chocolate, chopped
¾ cup (185 ml) hot water
1 tablespoon golden syrup
2 teaspoons vanilla extract
1 cup (160 g) dark brown sugar
2 eggs, at room temperature
2 cups (320 g) self-raising flour

1. Preheat the oven to 160°C (320°F) fan forced. Grease an 18 cm (7 inch) round cake tin and line the base with baking paper.

2. Combine the butter, chocolate, hot water, golden syrup and vanilla in a saucepan. Cook over low heat, whisking constantly, until smooth and well combined. Remove from the heat and set aside until lukewarm.

3. Meanwhile, use electric beaters to whisk the brown sugar and eggs in a large mixing bowl until pale and creamy. Whisk in the chocolate mixture until well combined. Add the flour and whisk until combined.

4. Pour the batter into the cake tin. Bake for 55 minutes or until a skewer inserted into the centre of the cake comes out almost clean. (The centre will be sticky, but will come together once cooled.) Cool completely in the tin, then cover the tin with plastic wrap and refrigerate for 30 minutes.

5. Remove the chilled cake from the tin. Use a long, thin knife to cut the cake horizontally into three even layers. Set aside until assembly.

CHOCOLATE GANACHE

300 ml (10½ fl oz) single (pure) cream
600 g (1 lb 5 oz) good-quality dark or milk chocolate, chopped

PEANUT BUTTER GANACHE
½ cup (140 g) peanut butter
Icing (confectioners') sugar, to taste

1. Pour the cream into a small saucepan and bring to a rolling boil (there should be bubbles all over the surface, not just around the edge). Remove from the heat and add the chocolate, stirring until there are no lumps.

2. Set the ganache aside overnight at room temperature to thicken.

3. To make the peanut butter ganache, take out 1 cup (250 ml) of the chocolate ganache. Using electric beaters, beat the ganache with the peanut butter until fluffy. Beat in the icing sugar, to taste.

ASSEMBLY AND DECORATION

1 cocktail skewer

2 giant marshmallows

100 g (3½ oz) white chocolate melts, melted

Mini white and yellow jellybeans (about 20 of each)

Assorted fruit-shaped gummy candies

3 wooden skewers

1 tinned apricot half, drained

½ cup (20 g) Cocoa Bombs cereal

5 gummy raspberries, roughly chopped

1 wire rack, about 18 cm (7 inch) diameter

2 chocolate-coated McVitie's Digestives biscuits

1. Working on a cake turntable or lazy Susan, secure the bottom layer of cake onto a cake plate or board with a dollop of ganache and then gently twist in place. Use an offset spatula to cover the top of the cake with a 1 cm (½ inch) layer of the peanut butter ganache, spreading it right to the edge. If the ganache is too thick, gently reheat it to a more workable consistency.

2. Place the second layer of cake on top and add another layer of peanut butter ganache. Place the last cake layer on top.

3. Using an offset spatula and a cake scraper, gently crumb coat the entire cake with a thin layer of chocolate ganache (see page 240), reheating the ganache if needed. Carefully smooth the side until the desired finish is achieved. Chill in the refrigerator for 20 minutes.

4. Apply another layer of chocolate ganache to the chilled cake and use an offset spatula to smooth the side and top (see page 241) – or you can use a cake scraper for a smoother finish.

5. To make the corn cob, insert a cocktail skewer into a marshmallow and cover the outside with melted white chocolate. Press the jelly beans into the chocolate. Allow to set.

6. To make the kebabs, thread various gummy candies and marshmallow slices onto the wooden skewers.

7. To make the egg, pat the apricot half dry with paper towel. Dollop some melted white chocolate onto a tray lined with baking paper and spread it into the shape of a fried egg white. Gently shake the tray to create a smooth surface. Gently press the apricot into the chocolate. Allow to set.

8. Press the Cocoa Bombs onto the cake and add some chopped raspberry and red fruit gummies. Place the wire rack on top. Arrange the corn cob, kebabs, egg and chocolate biscuits on top and... YOU BEAUT!

Decorating Tips

- You can also bake the cake in three 18 cm (7 inch) cake layer tins and reduce the cooking time to about 30 minutes.
- Use dark or milk chocolate in the ganache – I prefer dark chocolate!
- You could use Tic Tacs instead of the mini jellybeans to make the corn.
- You can use maraschino cherries instead of the red gummies.
- Speed up the cooling time for the ganache by placing it in the fridge or freezer and stirring every 20–30 minutes until the desired consistency is reached.

Press mini white and yellow jellybeans into a marshmallow covered with melted white chocolate to make the corn cob.

Spread the white chocolate to resemble the shape of a fried egg white, then press the apricot half on top.

It's a good idea to make a spare fried egg in case one of them breaks when you're decorating the cake.

Create the glowing coals of the barbecue by pressing the Cocoa Bombs and chopped red gummies into the ganache.

CHAPTER 3

ADVANCED AUSTRALIAN FARE

Now you're ready to do AMAZING! You've mastered the basics; you've learnt the tricks. Have confidence in yourself and your skills and step up to the oven. There are few things in life that feel as great as baking a smash-hit cake for people you love.

THE MINING MAGNATE

They say pressure creates precious stones, but I reckon all you need is chocolate!
We've got a pretty few mining millionaires in Australia – historically, we are the world's largest exporter of coal, iron ore, lead, diamonds, zinc and zirconium (my next band name); second largest exporters of gold and uranium (my first band name), and third largest of aluminium (the baker's best friend). Mining has been a good friend to some, but has had an environmental impact too – shall we settle our political differences over a piece of cake then?

SERVES 12–14

MILLIONAIRE'S CAKE (IT'S RICH!)

½ cup (55 g) cocoa powder
1 cup (250 ml) boiling water
4 eggs, at room temperature
1½ cups (330 g) caster sugar
½ cup (115 g) melted coconut oil
1 teaspoon vanilla extract
1¼ cups (200 g) self-raising flour

SYRUP
1½ cups (375 ml) evaporated milk
1 cup (220 g) caster sugar
2 teaspoons vanilla extract
1½ tablespoons brandy (optional –
    see tips)

1. Preheat the oven to 160°C (320°F) fan forced. Grease four 15 cm (6 inch) round cake layer tins and line with baking paper.

2. Dissolve the cocoa in the boiling water and set aside to cool.

3. Separate the eggs. Beat the egg whites until stiff peaks form. Set aside.

4. Using an electric mixer, beat the egg yolks and sugar until light and fluffy. Add the cooled cocoa mixture and beat well. Add the coconut oil and vanilla and beat well.

5. Sift in the flour and beat until just combined, being careful not to over-mix. Very gently fold in the stiffly beaten egg whites.

6. Divide the batter evenly among the cake tins and bake for 20–30 minutes or until a skewer inserted into the centre of each cake comes out clean.

7. While the cakes are baking, make the syrup. Combine the evaporated milk, sugar, vanilla and brandy, if using, in a saucepan and bring to the boil. Reduce the heat to a simmer and gently stir until the sugar has dissolved.

8. Remove the cooked cakes from the oven. Prick all over the top of each cake with a fork. Pour the syrup over the cakes. Leave the cakes in the tins to cool completely.

WHITE CHOCOLATE SWISS MERINGUE BUTTERCREAM

1½ cups (330 g) caster sugar
8 large egg whites
200 g (7 oz) good-quality white chocolate, chopped
2 cups (500 g) unsalted butter, softened
1 teaspoon vanilla bean paste

1. Put the sugar and egg whites in a heatproof glass bowl. Set the bowl over a pan of gently simmering water and whisk until the sugar has dissolved and the mixture is slightly warm to the touch. Remove from the heat.
2. Using an electric mixer fitted with the whisk attachment, beat on high speed until the mixture has formed stiff and glossy peaks (about 10–15 minutes).
3. Meanwhile, melt the chocolate using either the microwave or double-boiler method (see page 245). Remove from the heat and keep warm.
4. Add the butter to the meringue in three batches, beating until incorporated after each addition. Beat in the melted chocolate. Add the vanilla and beat until fluffy, then beat on low speed to eliminate air bubbles. Cover the bowl with plastic wrap and set aside in a cool place until needed.

WHITE CHOCOLATE GEMS

500 g (1 lb 2 oz) white chocolate melts
Blue, green, pink, purple and orange oil-based chocolate colouring
Silicone gem/jewel moulds
Edible lustre dust

1. Working in batches, melt the white chocolate using either the microwave or double-boiler method. Tint the chocolate to the desired colours and spoon into a piping bag. Cut off the tip and pipe the coloured chocolate into the moulds. Refrigerate for about 1 hour or until completely set.
2. Carefully pop the gems out of the moulds and lightly dust them with lustre dust using a clean dusting brush.

ASSEMBLY AND DECORATION

1. Working on a cake turntable or lazy Susan, secure the bottom layer of cake onto a cake stand or board with a dollop of buttercream and then gently twist in place. Use an offset spatula to cover the top of the cake with a 5 mm (¼ inch) layer of buttercream, spreading it right to the edge.
2. Place the second cake layer on top and repeat the layering process until the last cake layer is added.
3. Using an offset spatula and a cake scraper, crumb coat the entire cake with a thin layer of buttercream (see page 240). Carefully smooth the side until the desired finish is achieved. Chill in the refrigerator for 20 minutes.
4. Apply a final thick layer of buttercream all over the cake and use the cake scraper and offset spatula to smooth the side and top (see page 241).
5. Using the picture on page 177 as a guide, decorate the cake with the chocolate gems.

STORAGE

- Store the cake at room temperature in a dry place until serving. The cake can be stored in an airtight container at room temperature for 2–3 days. It can also be refrigerated for up to 5 days.

- The chocolate gems can be made ahead and stored in an airtight container in a cool place. Dust them with the lustre dust just before decorating the cake.

Decorating Tips

- You can use 1½ tablespoons espresso instead of the brandy to make the syrup for the cake.
- You can also use pasteurised egg whites from a carton to make Swiss meringue buttercream. You won't need to whisk the sugar into the egg whites over a pan of simmering water — simply place the sugar and egg whites directly into the mixer.
- The silicone gem/jewel moulds and oil-based chocolate colouring are available from cake decorating stores and online.

The easiest and neatest way to fill the moulds with the coloured chocolate is using a piping bag.

Use a clean dusting brush to add a light coating of edible lustre dust to the chocolate gems.

MURIEL'S WEDDING CAKE

'I'm a bride. I'm supposed to be euphoric!' Don't fret: this keeper of a vegan recipe is here to help calm any wedding party nerves, whether you know your partner or not. The decoration might look a little over the top, but it's important to reach for the stars if you want your life to be as good as an ABBA song. I recommend you halve the lemon cake ingredients and bake in two batches as described below (unless you have a huge commercial oven) with a 13 cm, 18 cm and 25 cm cake in each batch. By the end of the baking adventure you should have six cakes: two of each different size.

SERVES 115–120

LEMON CAKES

Cooking oil spray
2.5 kg (5 lb 8 oz) self-raising flour
1.5 kg (3 lb 5 oz) caster sugar
4 tablespoons baking powder
Grated zest of 8 lemons
10 cups (2.5 litres) non-dairy milk
4 cups (1 litre) vegetable oil or
    melted coconut oil
50 ml (1½ fl oz) vanilla extract
200 ml (7 fl oz) warm elderflower
    syrup (see page 184)

1. Preheat the oven to 170°C (340°F) fan forced. Grease a 13 cm (5 inch), 18 cm (7 inch) and 25 cm (10 inch) deep round cake tin with cooking oil spray. Line the tins with baking paper.

2. Halve the lemon cake ingredients and set one half aside for the second batch of cakes. In a very large bowl, mix together the flour, sugar, baking powder and lemon zest.

3. Add the non-dairy milk, oil and vanilla in three batches, gently mixing in between each batch until everything is combined.

4. Divide the batter among the cake tins, filling each one to the same depth. Tap the tins on the bench to pop any air bubbles.

5. Bake the cakes for 45 minutes, then remove the small cake and insert a skewer into the centre. If the skewer comes out clean, allow the cake to cool. If not, return the cake to the oven and test again every 5 minutes. The larger cakes will take longer to bake – around 1 hour for the 18 cm cake and 1 hour and 20 minutes for the 25 cm cake – but be sure to keep an eye on them, as all ovens are different.

6. Once all the cakes are baked, use a pastry brush to cover them with a generous layer of warm elderflower syrup. Reserve the remaining syrup to use when assembling the cakes.

7. Allow the cakes to cool in the tins before transferring them to a wire rack to cool completely. Wrap the cakes in plastic wrap until needed.

8. Use the remaining ingredients to bake another three cakes, using freshly greased and lined cake tins.

ELDERFLOWER SYRUP

350 ml (12 fl oz) elderflower cordial
300 g (10½ oz) caster sugar

1. Pour the cordial into a saucepan. Add the sugar and stir over low heat until dissolved. Bring to the boil, then reduce the heat and simmer for a few minutes until the syrup is slightly thickened. Remove from the heat and set aside.

LEMON AND ELDERFLOWER CURD

175 ml (5½ fl oz) lemon juice
75 ml (2¼ fl oz) elderflower cordial
½ cup (125 ml) water
250 g (9 oz) caster sugar
65 g (2¼ oz) cornflour
150 ml (5 fl oz) soya cream
1 tablespoon vegan butter
1 pinch salt

1. Combine the lemon juice, cordial, water and sugar in a small bowl.
2. Put the cornflour in a small saucepan. Stir in the lemon mixture, 1 tablespoon at a time. Bring to the boil over medium heat and cook, stirring, for 1 minute or until thickened. Reduce the heat to low and stir. The mixture should be thick and glossy.
3. Remove from the heat and stir in the soya cream, vegan butter and salt. Allow to cool completely. Refrigerate in an airtight container until needed.

VEGAN SWISS MERINGUE BUTTERCREAM

4 cups (1 litre) liquid drained from tinned chickpeas (about 5 cans)
3 cups (660 g) caster sugar
1½ teaspoons cream of tartar
2 cups (280 g) icing (confectioners') sugar, sifted
500 g (1 lb 2 oz) high-ratio solid vegetable shortening (see tips)
900 g (2 lb) vegan butter, softened
1¼ tablespoons vanilla bean paste

1. Combine the chickpea liquid and sugar in a large saucepan and bring to a full boil. Boil for 5 minutes, then transfer to the large bowl of an electric mixer to cool completely.
2. Fit the whisk attachment to the electric mixer and whip the cooled mixture (at this point it is known as 'aquafaba') on high speed until it is thick and glossy and has firm peaks. This will take about 15 minutes.
3. Combine the cream of tartar with 1 tablespoon of the icing sugar and add it to the whipped, firm meringue. Continue whipping while you gradually add the remaining icing sugar.
4. Add the vegetable shortening and vegan butter and continue whipping on high speed until light and fluffy. Add the vanilla and whip until combined.

ASSEMBLY AND DECORATION

8 wooden cake dowels or plastic
   bubble tea straws
15 cm (6 inch) round cardboard cake
   stacking board
10 cm (4 inch) round cardboard cake
   stacking board
Piping gel
1 cup (140 g) fresh blackberries
Edible purple glitter
Cake decorators' rose spirit
Edible gold lustre dust
1 cup (140 g) fresh blueberries
3 bunches of tiny grapes
6 small figs
Edible fresh flowers (see tips)

1. Use a long, thin knife to divide each of the cakes horizontally into two even layers.

2. Working on a cake turntable or lazy Susan, secure the bottom layer of the 25 cm cake onto a cake board or plate with a dollop of buttercream and then gently twist in place. Brush with a small amount of elderflower syrup and cover with a thin layer of lemon and elderflower curd. Use an offset spatula to cover the cake with a 5 mm (¼ inch) layer of buttercream, spreading it right to the edge of the cake.

3. Place the second cake layer on top and repeat the layering process until the last 25 cm cake layer is added.

4. Use an offset spatula and a cake scraper to gently crumb coat the cake with a thin layer of buttercream (see page 240). Carefully smooth the side until the desired finish is achieved. Use an offset spatula to smooth the top of the cake by gently pulling inwards from the outer edge into the centre, cleaning the excess buttercream off the spatula with each scrape. Chill the cake in the refrigerator for 10 minutes or until firm.

5. Apply a final layer of buttercream all over the cake and carefully smooth the side with a cake scraper. Use the offset spatula to smooth the top of the cake (see page 241). Return the cake to the fridge for about 1 hour.

6. I usually just estimate where the cake on top will sit but you can be more precise by taking a cardboard cake board or tin the same size as the next tier to be added on top. Place it in the middle of the cake and lightly mark the outline with a toothpick or knife.

7. Take four cake dowels and insert one into the cake, inside the markings. Mark the height of the cake with your thumb, remove the dowel and mark the height with a pen. Cut the dowel with scissors or a serrated knife and use it as a guide when cutting the remaining three dowels. Insert the four cake dowels.

8. Place the first layer of the 18 cm cake on the 15 cm cake board. Layer, fill, frost and chill the cake as for the 25 cm cake. When firm, add the cake dowels as above, using three dowels instead of four.

9. Place the first layer of the 13 cm cake on the 10 cm cake board. Layer, fill, frost and chill the cake as before.

10. Use a large metal spatula or cake lifter to help carefully lift and guide the second tier on top of the first. Do the same with the third cake tier.

STORAGE

- This cake is best enjoyed at room temperature, so ensure it has been out of the refrigerator for at least 2 hours before serving. It can be refrigerated for up to 4 days or frozen (without the decorations) for up to 1–2 months.

- The cakes can be baked ahead and refrigerated (covered in plastic wrap) in an airtight container for up to 2 days. They can also be frozen for up to 1 month. Thaw them overnight in the fridge before decorating.

- The vegan Swiss meringue buttercream can be made up to 2 weeks ahead and refrigerated. Bring it to room temperature and then whip it to a workable consistency before using.

11. To secure the cakes and make sure the tiers won't slide off, take a long wooden dowel, slightly shorter than the cake. Sharpen one end with a clean sharpener and, with the help of a clean hammer, carefully drive it down through all the layers until it reaches the base. Use an extra dowel to help push it all the way down. Mask the hole created on top with buttercream and fix any gaps or blemishes between the tiers.

12. Thin the piping gel with a little hot water. Brush the blackberries with the gel and decorate with edible glitter.

13. To make edible metallic paint, mix a small amount of cake decorators' rose spirit with the lustre dust. Brush the paint onto the fruits.

14. Using the picture on page 183 as a guide, decorate the cake with an arrangement of glitzed-up and fresh fruits and edible fresh flowers (it's best to do this on the day of the wedding or other special occasion).

Decorating Tips

- For an even sturdier vegan Swiss meringue buttercream, refrigerate the drained chickpea liquid overnight, which will allow it to thicken and more closely resemble egg whites.

- High-ratio solid vegetable shortening, such as CK Products or Crisco brand, give stability and smoothness to the buttercream. They can be found at cake decorating stores and online.

- Edible fresh flowers are available from specialty ingredient stores and farmers' markets.

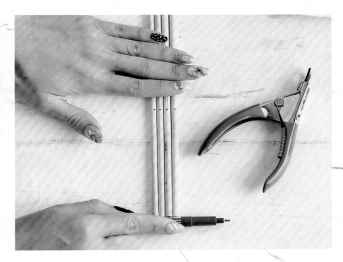

Mark the height of the dowels with a pen and then cut to size using clean nail clippers, scissors or a serrated knife.

Insert the dowels into the bottom layer of the cake, using an extra dowel to push them right to the bottom.

Use a large metal spatula or cake lifter to help lift the second cake tier on top of the first.

To secure the cakes, hammer a sharpened dowel through all of the layers until it reaches the base.

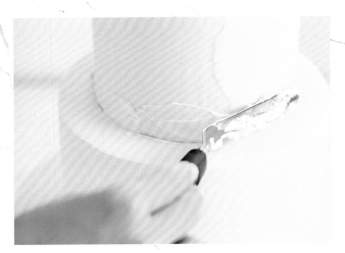

Use a small offset spatula to mask the hole on top of the cake with buttercream, and fill in any gaps or blemishes between the tiers.

Once all of the tiers are in place, use a small cake scraper to smooth the side of each tier.

GREAT BARRIER REEF CAKE

Coral that's visible from outer space? Yep, we have that here in Australia. The Great Barrier Reef is the largest living thing on Earth, and can be seen from space if you're looking out of the window of your rocket. Bursting with the world's greatest collection of ecological biodiversity, it was named a UNESCO World Heritage Site in 1981 and is considered by many to be one of the wonders of the world. Let your imagination run wild with these decorations: there are still countless species of deliciously other-worldly marvels to be discovered in the deep.

SERVES 18–20

CARAMEL SPONGE CAKE

6 eggs, at room temperature
1⅔ cups (270 g) brown sugar
1½ cups (210 g) cornflour
1½ teaspoons cream of tartar
¾ teaspoon bicarbonate of soda (baking soda)

1. Preheat the oven to 170°C (340°F) fan forced. Grease two 18 cm (7 inch) deep round cake tins and line the bases with baking paper.
2. Using an electric mixer, beat the eggs and brown sugar for 10 minutes or until thick and creamy.
3. Sift the dry ingredients together three times, then sift over the egg mixture and gently fold together, being careful not to over-mix.
4. Divide the batter evenly between the cake tins. Bake for 25 minutes or until the centre of each cake springs back when lightly pressed. Leave in the tins for 15 minutes, then turn out onto a wire rack to cool completely.

VANILLA BEAN SWISS MERINGUE BUTTERCREAM

1½ cups (330 g) caster sugar
8 large egg whites
2 cups (500 g) unsalted butter, softened
1 teaspoon vanilla bean paste
Turquoise gel food colouring

1. Put the sugar and egg whites in a heatproof glass bowl. Set the bowl over a pan of gently simmering water and whisk until the sugar has dissolved and the mixture is slightly warm to the touch. Remove from the heat.
2. Using an electric mixer fitted with the whisk attachment, beat on high speed until the mixture has formed stiff and glossy peaks (about 10–15 minutes).
3. Add the butter in three batches, beating until incorporated after each addition. Add the vanilla and beat until fluffy.
4. Set aside 5 tablespoons of the buttercream to assemble the chocolate clam shells. Colour the remaining buttercream turquoise. Cover the bowls with plastic wrap and set aside in a cool place until needed.

CHOCOLATE CORAL

300 g (10½ oz) white chocolate melts
Purple oil-based or powdered chocolate colouring
2 kg (4 lb 8 oz) ice cubes
Edible lustre dust or lustre spray

1. Melt the chocolate using either the microwave or double-boiler method (see page 245). Tint the chocolate with the purple chocolate colouring to the desired shade.

2. Put the ice cubes in a deep bowl. Pour the melted chocolate over the ice and shake to settle.

3. Allow the chocolate to harden, then carefully remove it from the bowl in one piece. Place on a wire rack over a tray to collect the melting ice. Leave the ice to melt completely, revealing an organic coral shape. Allow the chocolate coral to dry completely.

4. Put the chocolate coral on a tray or clean tea towel and decorate with lustre dust or spray.

SEA SHELLS

200 g (7 oz) white chocolate melts
Pink, blue, orange, green and purple oil-based or powdered chocolate colouring
Sea shell moulds
5 white candy-coated chocolate pearls

1. Working in batches, melt the white chocolate using either the microwave or double-boiler method. Tint the chocolate to the desired colour and spoon into a piping bag with the tip cut off at 3 mm (⅛ inch). Pipe the chocolate into the sea shell moulds and tap on the bench to remove air pockets. Refrigerate until the chocolate is firm and has contracted from the sides of the moulds.

2. Carefully remove the chocolates from the moulds. Store in an airtight container in a cool place.

3. To make chocolate clams, put the reserved buttercream in a piping bag with the tip cut off at 2 cm (¾ inch). Pipe a little buttercream onto a clam half and place another clam half on top. Embed a white candy-coated chocolate in the middle. Refrigerate until needed.

EASY SUGAR GLASS SHARDS

100 g (3½ oz) hard-boiled coloured candies

1. Preheat the oven to 160°C (320°F). Line a baking tray with a silicone mat or baking paper.

2. Put the candies in a resealable plastic bag and smash into smaller pieces using a rolling pin, hammer or pestle.

3. Spread the crushed candies on the tray. Bake for about 7 minutes or until completely melted. Remove from the oven and allow to cool completely, then break into shards of various sizes. Store in an airtight container.

ASSEMBLY AND DECORATION

½ cup (150 g) lemon curd or
  salted caramel (page 246
  or store-bought)
White candy-coated chocolate balls
  in assorted sizes
Large pink candy-coated chocolate
  balls (see tips)

1. Use a long, thin knife to divide each cake into two even horizontal layers.

2. Working on a cake turntable or lazy Susan, secure the bottom layer of cake onto a cake stand or board with a dollop of turquoise buttercream and gently twist in place. Use an offset spatula to spread a thin layer of lemon curd or salted caramel over the cake, then cover with a 5–10 mm (¼–½ inch) layer of buttercream, spreading it right to the edge.

3. Place the second cake layer on top and repeat the layering process until the last cake layer is added.

4. Using an offset spatula and a cake scraper, gently crumb coat the entire cake with a thin layer of turquoise buttercream (see page 240). Carefully smooth the side until the desired finish is achieved. Chill in the refrigerator for 15–20 minutes.

5. Apply a final layer of turquoise buttercream all over the cake and use the cake scraper and offset spatula to smooth the side and top (see page 241).

6. Using the picture on page 188 as a guide, decorate the cake with the chocolate coral, chocolate sea shells, chocolate clams, chocolate balls and sugar glass shards.

Decorating Tips

- You can also use pasteurised egg whites from a carton to make Swiss meringue buttercream. You won't need to whisk the sugar into the egg whites over a pan of simmering water – simply place the sugar and egg whites directly into the mixer.
- The sea shell moulds used to make the chocolate shells are available from cake decorating stores and online.
- You can use either couverture or compound chocolate to make the chocolate coral.
- I crushed yellow, pink and green lollipops for the sugar glass shards.
- Look for assorted sizes of candy-coated chocolate balls online or in cake decorating stores. I used Darrell Lea Strawberry Sensation balls for the pink chocolate balls.

STORAGE

This cake is best served at room temperature. It can be refrigerated for up to 4 days.

Pour the coloured chocolate over the bowl of ice cubes to form the chocolate coral.

Pipe the coloured chocolate into an assortment of sea shell moulds to make the decorations for the cake.

Once the chocolate has completely set, carefully remove the chocolates from the moulds.

Sandwich a pair of clam shells together with buttercream and add one of the candy-coated chocolate pearls.

SHOWGIRL KYLIE CAKE

The Singing Budgie turned Princess of Pop, our triumphant showgirl, Kylie Minogue,
is a *Neighbours*-made international superstar, songstress, actress, activist and style icon.
The Brits might try to claim her, but we consider Kylie as Australian as the smell of eucalyptus
or a sausage sizzle on a hot day. Here we celebrate Our Kylie, in all her glittery, deliciously
Dolly Varden-esque glory. Feel free to style Kylie in other excitingly edible ensembles.

SERVES 16

CINNAMON APPLE CAKE

1½ cups (240 g) brown sugar

⅓ cup (80 ml) vegetable oil

1 teaspoon vanilla extract

3 eggs, at room temperature

2½ cups (400 g) self-raising flour

1 cup (250 ml) buttermilk, at room
  temperature

1 teaspoon bicarbonate of soda
  (baking soda)

1 teaspoon ground cinnamon

1½ cups (200 g) chopped apple

1. Preheat the oven to 160°C (320°F) fan forced. Grease a Dolly Varden cake tin.
2. Using an electric mixer, beat the brown sugar, oil and vanilla. Slowly beat in the eggs, one at a time.
3. Add the flour and buttermilk in three batches, mixing until combined. Add the bicarbonate of soda and cinnamon. Fold in the chopped apple and mix until combined.
4. Pour the batter into the cake tin. Bake for 1 hour or until a skewer inserted into the centre of the cake comes out clean. Leave to cool in the tin for at least 1 hour before turning out onto a wire rack to cool completely.

RASPBERRY CREAM CHEESE FROSTING

⅓ cup (80 g) unsalted butter,
  softened

500 g (1 lb 2 oz) cream cheese,
  softened

1 teaspoon vanilla bean paste

1 teaspoon lemon juice

1½ cups (210 g) icing (confectioners')
  sugar

20 g (¾ oz) freeze-dried raspberry
  powder (see tips)

Pink food colouring

1. Using an electric mixer, beat the butter on medium speed until creamy. Add the cream cheese, vanilla and lemon juice and beat until creamy. Gradually increase the speed to high and continue beating until light and fluffy.
2. Gradually sift in the icing sugar, beating on low speed until well combined. Add the raspberry powder and mix until blended, then increase the speed to high and beat until well combined and smooth. While beating, add the pink colouring until the desired shade is reached.
3. Chill the frosting in the fridge, if needed, until it has firmed to a workable consistency for filling the cake layers.

ASSEMBLY AND DECORATION

3 cups (150 g) natural coconut flakes
Pink edible colouring spray
1 doll with legs 'popped' off
16 pink and white craft feathers
Hot glue gun or double-sided tape
Adhesive craft gems

1. Using a long, thin knife, trim the cake so that it will sit level. Divide the cake into four horizontal layers.

2. Working on a cake turntable or lazy Susan, secure the bottom layer of cake onto a cake board or large serving plate with a dollop of frosting and then gently twist in place. Use an offset spatula to apply a layer of frosting to the top of the cake, spreading it right to the edge.

3. Place the second cake layer on top and repeat the layering process until the last cake layer is added.

4. Using an offset spatula, crumb coat the cake with a thin layer of frosting (see page 240). Chill the cake in the refrigerator for 20 minutes to firm.

5. Apply a final generous layer of frosting all over the cake and use the offset spatula or a small cake scraper to smooth the side and top (see page 241). The frosting doesn't need to be completely smooth as it will be covered.

6. Using the pictures as a guide, decorate the side of the cake with coconut flakes to create a ruffled effect. Reserve the remaining coconut flakes.

7. To create a pink ombre effect, start from the bottom of the cake and spray with pink edible colouring. Use a lighter touch and thinner concentration of colouring as you work up towards the middle of the cake. Stop spraying completely once you reach the top third of the cake.

8. Tie the doll's hair into a bun. Trim the feathers to place around the doll's head and use the hot glue gun or double-sided tape to stick them in place.

9. Stick the adhesive gems around the doll's neck and hairline. Place strips of adhesive gems along her arms and around her torso to create a bedazzling showgirl costume. Use a little hot glue to secure the gems, if necessary.

10. Carefully place the doll on the cake. If needed, pipe a 'dam' of left-over frosting on top of the cake to hold her in position. Decorate the doll's back with a peacock-tail arrangement of feathers. Insert the remaining coconut flakes around the base of her torso.

Decorating Tips

- Replace the raspberry powder with ⅓ cup (80 ml) puréed raspberries or ⅓ cup (110 g) 100% fruit raspberry jam if you like.
- If you want to keep the doll's legs intact, wrap them in plastic wrap. You'll need to hollow out part of the cake to allow room for the legs. If you'd prefer to keep the glue away from her hair, you can tightly wrap her hair in foil.
- Natural coconut flakes are available in health food stores.
- Pink edible colouring spray is available in cake decorating stores.
- You can buy adhesive craft gems in craft stores.

Use an offset spatula to apply a layer of raspberry cream cheese frosting to the bottom layer of cake.

Place the second cake layer on top and add another layer of frosting, spreading it right to the edge.

Add the next layer of cake and frosting, gently pressing them together and ensuring they are sitting level.

Decorate the frosted cake with the natural coconut flakes to create a ruffled effect.

Spray the cake with the edible colouring, using a lighter touch and thinner concentration of colouring as you work upwards.

Carefully place the doll on the cake, piping a 'dam' of frosting to hold her in position, if needed.

THE BLACK OPAL

Black opals are the most valuable form of this precious stone and can be found only in Australia and North America. The stone has a dark grey or black background, in which a fiery display of glowing dark green, gold, blue, black or pale violet can be seen. Being guardians of such an impressive natural resource, it is only fitting that we create an equally eye-catching cake in its name. The glossy mirror glaze is a traditional technique used to decorate mousse cakes (known as entremets) and pastries. Giving the glaze a quick blast of heat with a hair dryer creates an out-of-this-world effect, reminiscent of the flashes of metallic colour seen in the black opals.

SERVES 12

DARK CHOCOLATE SEA SALT CAKE

Cooking oil spray
1 cup (175 g) chopped dark
   chocolate
1 cup (230 g) coconut oil
2½ cups (400 g) self-raising flour
1½ cups (330 g) caster sugar
½ cup (55 g) cocoa powder
½ teaspoon bicarbonate of soda
   (baking soda)
½ teaspoon sea salt
4 large eggs, at room temperature
1½ cups (375 ml) milk, at room
   temperature
1 teaspoon vanilla extract

1. Preheat the oven to 160°C (320°F) fan forced. Grease three 18 cm (7 inch) round cake tins with cooking oil spray. Line the tins with baking paper.

2. Melt the chocolate and coconut oil using either the microwave or double-boiler method (see page 245). Stir until combined. Set the mixture aside to cool to room temperature.

3. Using an electric mixer fitted with the paddle attachment, gently fold the dry ingredients together until combined.

4. With the mixer on low speed, slowly add the chocolate mixture to the dry ingredients. Beat in the eggs, one at a time, then beat in the milk and vanilla. Mix until combined.

5. Divide the batter among the cake tins. Bake for 45 minutes or until a skewer inserted into the centre of the cakes comes out clean. Leave the cakes to cool in the tins for at least 1 hour before turning out onto a wire rack to cool completely.

DARK CHOCOLATE SWISS MERINGUE BUTTERCREAM

1½ cups (330 g) caster sugar
8 large egg whites
300 g (10½ oz) good-quality dark
  chocolate, chopped
2 cups (500 g) unsalted butter,
  softened
1 teaspoon vanilla bean paste

1. Put the sugar and egg whites in a heatproof glass bowl. Set the bowl over a pan of gently simmering water and whisk until the sugar has dissolved and the mixture is slightly warm to the touch. Remove from the heat.

2. Using an electric mixer fitted with the whisk attachment, beat on high speed until the mixture has formed stiff and glossy peaks (about 10–15 minutes).

3. Meanwhile, melt the chocolate using either the microwave or double-boiler method (see page 245). Remove from the heat and keep warm.

4. Add the butter to the meringue in three batches, beating until incorporated after each addition. (Don't be alarmed if it appears curdled – it will become light and fluffy with continued whipping, I promise!) Beat in the chocolate. Add the vanilla and beat until fluffy, then beat on low speed to eliminate air bubbles. Cover the bowl with plastic wrap and set aside in a cool place until needed.

GLAZE

12 g (¼ oz) gold-strength gelatine
  sheets
150 g (5½ oz) good-quality white
  chocolate, chopped
110 ml (3½ fl oz) water
⅔ cup (150 g) caster sugar
100 g (3½ oz) glucose syrup
100 g (3½ oz) sweetened condensed
  milk
Black, purple, blue and green gel
  food colouring

1. Soak the gelatine sheets in iced water for 20 minutes.

2. Meanwhile, put the white chocolate in a heatproof bowl.

3. Combine the water, sugar and glucose syrup in a saucepan and bring to the boil. Remove from the heat and stir in the condensed milk and drained gelatine sheets.

4. Pour the hot sugar mixture over the chocolate. Mix with a stick blender until the chocolate is melted and smooth (or you can mix thoroughly with a spoon), being careful not to create air bubbles.

5. Divide the glaze among four bowls and tint each portion with one of the gel colours until the desired shade is reached.

6. Cover the surface of the glaze with plastic wrap and allow it to cool to around 35°C (95°F).

7. Pour all the glaze colours into one jug (being careful not to over-mix or blend) and use immediately. (Don't fret if the glaze cools before you are able to use it – gently re-heat it in the microwave in 5–10 second bursts, stirring in between.)

ASSEMBLY AND DECORATION

1. Working on a cake turntable or lazy Susan, secure the bottom layer of cake onto a cake board with a dollop of chocolate buttercream and then gently twist in place. Use an offset spatula to cover the top of the cake with a 5 mm (¼ inch) layer of buttercream, spreading it right to the edge.

2. Place the second layer of cake on top and repeat the layering process. Add the final cake layer.

3. Using an offset spatula and a cake scraper, gently crumb coat the entire cake with a thin layer of buttercream (see page 240). Carefully smooth the side and top until the desired finish is achieved. Chill in the refrigerator for 10 minutes or until firm.

4. Use an offset spatula to roughly apply a thick layer of buttercream all over the cake and use the cake scraper and offset spatula to smooth the side and top (see page 241).

5. Chill the cake in the freezer for at least 1 hour.

6. Gently remove the chilled cake from the cake board using a hot knife and a large spatula. Place on a cooling rack or an upturned 15 cm (6 inch) cake tin on top of a large baking tray to catch the run-off glaze.

7. Working quickly, pour the coloured glaze onto the centre of the cake, then work your way out to the edge. Once the cake is completely covered, use a hair dryer to give the surface a quick blast of heat – about 2 seconds – to create the marbled effect. Let the glaze continue to drip and set for about 3 minutes, then carefully transfer the cake onto a cake board. Allow the cake to thaw in the refrigerator for at least 1 hour, then leave it at room temperature for at least 1 hour before serving.

Gently transfer the chilled, frosted cake to a cooling rack and place on top of a baking tray, ready to catch the run-off glaze.

Pour all the glaze colours into a jug, being careful not to over-mix or blend the colours.

Working quickly, start pouring the coloured glaze onto the centre of the frosted cake.

Continue pouring the coloured glaze until the top and side of the cake are completely covered.

Give the cake a quick blast of heat from a hair dryer to create a marbled effect, then leave to set.

Once the glaze is set, use two large spatulas to carefully transfer the cake onto a cake board.

'I STILL CALL AUSTRALIA HOME' WEDDING CAKE

Wedding cakes sit proudly on their pedestals, drawing all glances from the moment guests enter the room, tempting us during drawn-out speeches, mocking our table manners, until, FINALLY, dessert time. I've loved watching Aussie home-bakers put their own spin on the traditional wedding cake, especially Aussies living overseas who want to celebrate their home in the flavours and decoration. Make the chocolate waratah flowers in advance (up to a month is fine) and take your time baking the cake layers. You'll find it's not as intimidating as you might think to make advanced Australian fare.

SERVES 45—50

LEMON POPPY SEED CAKES

23 CM (9 INCH) CAKE
220 g (7¾ oz) unsalted butter, softened
1 cup (220 g) caster sugar
8 large eggs, at room temperature
3½ cups (360 g) almond meal
60 g (2¼ oz) poppy seeds
Grated zest and juice of 4 lemons
2 teaspoons vanilla extract
260 g (9¼ oz) self-raising flour, sifted

15 CM (6 INCH) CAKE
110 g (3¾ oz) unsalted butter, softened
½ cup (110 g) caster sugar
4 large eggs, at room temperature
1¾ cups (180 g) almond meal
30 g (1 oz) poppy seeds
Grated zest and juice of 2 lemons
1 teaspoon vanilla extract
130 g (4½ oz) self-raising flour, sifted

1. Preheat the oven to 160°C (320°F) fan forced. Grease one 23 cm (9 inch) and one 15 cm (6 inch) round spring-form cake tin. Line the tins with baking paper, with the paper extending 7.5 cm (3 inches) above the top of the tins to prevent the cakes from spilling over. Prepare and bake the cakes one at a time so that they rise evenly.

2. To prepare the 23 cm cake, use an electric mixer to beat the butter and sugar until light and creamy. Add the eggs, one at a time, beating well after each addition.

3. Gently fold in the almond meal, poppy seeds, lemon zest, lemon juice, vanilla and flour until just combined.

4. Spoon the batter into the cake tin. Bake for 1 hour 10 minutes or until the top of the cake is lightly golden. Cool in the tin for 1 hour (until the bottom of the tin is no longer warm to touch) before turning out onto a wire rack to cool completely.

5. Prepare the small cake using the same method and reducing the cooking time to 40 minutes.

6. Use a long, thin knife to carefully cut each cake into three horizontal layers. Cover with plastic wrap and set aside until needed.

RASPBERRY AND LEMON CREAM CHEESE FILLING

800 g (1 lb 12 oz) cream cheese,
    softened
150 g (5½ oz) unsalted butter,
    softened
30 g (1 oz) freeze-dried raspberry
    powder (see tips)
1 teaspoon vanilla bean paste
2 cups (280 g) icing (confectioners')
    sugar, sifted
2 teaspoons grated lemon zest
2 teaspoons lemon juice
3 teaspoons single (pure) cream
Pink gel food colouring

1. Using an electric mixer, beat the softened cream cheese on medium speed until smooth.

2. Add the butter, raspberry powder, vanilla, icing sugar, lemon zest, lemon juice and cream, and beat until light and fluffy. While beating, add the pink colouring until the desired shade is reached.

3. Cover the filling with plastic wrap. Refrigerate for 30 minutes, if needed, until it has firmed to a workable consistency for filling the cake layers.

WHITE CHOCOLATE SWISS MERINGUE BUTTERCREAM

1½ cups (330 g) caster sugar
8 large egg whites
300 g (10½ oz) good-quality white
    chocolate, chopped
2 cups (500 g) unsalted butter,
    softened
1 teaspoon vanilla bean paste
Red and pink gel food colouring

1. Put the sugar and egg whites in a heatproof glass bowl. Set the bowl over a pan of gently simmering water and whisk until the sugar has dissolved and the mixture is slightly warm to the touch. Remove from the heat.

2. Using an electric mixer fitted with the whisk attachment, beat on high speed until the mixture has formed stiff and glossy peaks (about 10–15 minutes).

3. Meanwhile, melt the chocolate using either the microwave or double-boiler method (see page 245). Remove from the heat and keep warm.

4. Add the butter to the meringue in three batches, beating until incorporated after each addition. (Don't be alarmed if it appears curdled — it will become light and fluffy with continued whipping, I promise!) Beat in the chocolate. Add the vanilla and beat until fluffy, then beat on low speed to eliminate air bubbles.

5. Transfer 1 cup of the buttercream to a bowl and mix in the red colouring. Put another 3 tablespoons of the buttercream in a small bowl and mix in the pink colouring. Cover all three bowls with plastic wrap and set aside in a cool place until needed.

Begin making the chocolate waratahs by filling two cavities of a semi-sphere mould with red chocolate.

Once the chocolate has set enough to form a shell, carefully pour the excess chocolate back into the bowl.

To make the petals, dip the tip of a long, sharp knife into the melted red chocolate and then press it onto the baking paper.

When the chocolate begins to set, quickly drape the baking paper over the rolling pin so that the petals set in a curved position.

CHOCOLATE WARATAH FLOWERS

500 g (1 lb 2 oz) white chocolate melts
Green and red oil-based chocolate colouring
1 semi-sphere silicone or polycarbonate mould with a diameter of 5 cm (2 inches)

1. Melt the chocolate using either the microwave or double-boiler method.

2. Put one-quarter of the melted chocolate into a smaller heatproof bowl and mix in the green colouring until the desired shade is reached. Colour the remaining white chocolate using the red colouring until the desired shade is reached.

3. To make the waratah centres, fill two cavities of the semi-sphere mould with the red chocolate. Allow the chocolate to sit for 5–10 minutes to form a 'shell'. Once a shell has formed, carefully pour the excess chocolate back into the bowl and scrape the mould with a cake scraper to clean the edges of the semi-sphere. Place the mould in the fridge for 15–20 minutes so that the chocolate contracts and will release easily from the mould. Invert the mould onto a hard surface and gently tap to release the semi-spheres.

4. To make the waratah petals, take a long rolling pin and cut a strip of baking paper that is the same length and circumference of the rolling pin. Secure the rolling pin onto the bench using sticky tape. Re-melt the red chocolate if needed. Working quickly, dip the tip of a long, sharp knife into the melted chocolate and press it onto the baking paper, pulling downwards to create a petal shape (it may take a few attempts to get the hang of it, but you can re-melt any dodgy petals!). Repeat until the chocolate begins to set, then quickly drape the baking paper over the rolling pin so that the petals will set in a curved position. Once the petals are completely set (this should take 10–15 minutes in a cool kitchen), carefully remove them from the paper and repeat with the remaining chocolate. You should end up with lots of petals – remember to allow for breakages during decorating.

5. Make the waratah leaves in the same way as the petals, but using the green chocolate. You won't need as many leaves as petals.

ASSEMBLY AND DECORATION

13 cm (5 inch) round cardboard cake
   stacking board
5 wooden cake dowels or plastic
   bubble tea straws

1. Working on a cake turntable or lazy Susan, secure the bottom layer of the 23 cm cake onto a cake board or plate with a dollop of buttercream and then gently twist in place. Use an offset spatula to cover the cake with a 5 mm (¼ inch) layer of raspberry and lemon cream cheese filling, spreading it right to the edge of the cake.

2. Place the second cake layer on top and repeat the layering process until the last 23 cm cake layer is added. If the filling is squeezing out between the layers, or if the cake feels unsteady (this will happen in warmer kitchens), refrigerate the cake until the filling has set before continuing the layering process.

3. Use an offset spatula and a cake scraper to gently crumb coat the cake with a thin layer of buttercream (see page 240). Carefully smooth the side until the desired finish is achieved. Use an offset spatula to smooth the top of the cake by gently pulling inwards from the outer edge into the centre, cleaning the excess buttercream off the spatula with each scrape. Chill the cake in the refrigerator for 10 minutes or until firm.

4. Use the offset spatula to roughly apply a thick layer of buttercream all over the cake. Using the cake scraper, smooth the side and top of the cake (see page 241). To create a water-coloured effect, use the spatula to apply strokes of red and pink buttercream (you won't need much) all over the cake. Use the cake scraper to once again smooth the side and top until the desired finish is achieved, scraping off the excess buttercream in the process. Save the remaining red buttercream to assemble the chocolate waratah flowers. Return the cake to the refrigerator for about 1 hour.

5. I usually just estimate where the cake on top will sit but you can be more precise by taking a cardboard cake board or tin the same size as the next tier to be added on top. Place it in the middle of the cake and lightly mark the outline with a toothpick or knife.

6. Referring to the instructions for stacking a tiered cake on page 242, take four cake dowels and insert one into the cake, inside the markings. Mark the height of the cake with your thumb, remove the dowel and mark the height with a pen. Cut the dowel with scissors or a serrated knife and use it as a guide to cut another three dowels. Insert the four cake dowels, then return the cake to the refrigerator.

7. Place the first layer of the 15 cm cake on the 13 cm cake board. Layer, fill, frost and chill the cake as for the 23 cm cake.

8. Use a large metal spatula or cake lifter to help carefully lift and guide the second cake tier on top of the first.

9. To secure the cakes and make sure the tiers won't slide off, trim the remaining dowel so that it is slightly shorter than the cake. Sharpen

one end with a clean sharpener and, with the help of a clean hammer, carefully drive it down through all the layers until it reaches the base. Use a spare dowel to help push it all the way down. Mask the hole created on top with buttercream and fix any gaps or blemishes between the tiers.

10. Using the picture on page 204 as a guide, gently press one of the chocolate semi-spheres onto the side of the bottom cake. Spoon the red buttercream into a piping bag with the end cut off at 3 mm (⅛ inch) and pipe around the edge of the semi-sphere to help secure it to the cake. Pipe small droplets of buttercream all over the semi-sphere to form the centre of the waratah. Pipe more red buttercream around the outside of the waratah centre, then very gently press a ring of chocolate petals into the buttercream. Pipe some more buttercream around the petals and add a second layer of petals. Repeat to make the second waratah on the side of the top cake.

11. Finally, place some of the leaves around each waratah. Decorate the base of the cake with any left-over chocolate petals or leaves to create a natural 'shedding' effect.

Decorating Tips

- You can also bake the cakes in separate layers, using three 6 inch (15 cm) tins and three 9 inch (23 cm) tins. Bake the smaller cakes for 20 minutes and the larger cakes for 30 minutes.
- If you can't find freeze-dried raspberry powder, use ½ cup (125 ml) puréed raspberries or ½ cup (160 g) 100% fruit raspberry jam.
- You can also use pasteurised egg whites from a carton to make Swiss meringue buttercream. You won't need to whisk the sugar into the egg whites over a pan of simmering water – simply place the sugar and egg whites directly into the mixer.

STORAGE

- The cake can be refrigerated for up to 5 days or frozen for up to 1 month. It is best served at room temperature for the best flavour and texture, so ensure it has been out of the refrigerator for at least 2 hours before serving. As with any cake containing chocolate decorations, beware of direct sunlight and warm weather!
- The lemon poppy seed cakes can be baked ahead and refrigerated (covered in plastic wrap) in an airtight container up to 3 days ahead or frozen for up to 1 month. Leave them to thaw in the refrigerator overnight before decorating.
- The petals, leaves and bulb centres for the chocolate waratahs can be made at least 1 month in advance. As with any chocolate decorations, store them in an airtight container, in a cool and dry place away from direct sunlight.

PRISCILLA, QUEEN OF THE DESSERT

It's time to get this cake show on the road. One of my all-time favourite productions is *The Adventures of Priscilla, Queen of the Desert*, the 1994 Australian road-trip comedy-drama by Stephan Elliott. It became a worldwide, Academy Award-winning hit and helped introduce LGBTQ themes to a mainstream audience. This cake is a celebration of inclusivity and our rich diversity as a nation. It should be served as a nod to being unashamedly vibrant and proud of who you are. Life is a sweet celebration and we are ALL invited to the party.

SERVES 12

RAINBOW SWIRL CAKE

¾ cup (180 g) unsalted butter, softened
1 cup (220 g) caster sugar
1 teaspoon vanilla extract
1 pinch salt
3 eggs, at room temperature
¾ cup (185 ml) milk, at room temperature
2 cups (320 g) self-raising flour, sifted
Pink, blue and yellow gel food colouring

1. Preheat the oven to 160°C (320°F) fan forced. Grease a Dolly Varden cake tin.
2. Using an electric mixer, beat the butter, sugar, vanilla and salt until fluffy. Add the eggs, one at a time, and beat until combined.
3. Add the milk and flour in three batches, stirring until combined.
4. Divide the mixture equally among three bowls and tint each portion with a different colour.
5. Spoon the batter into the cake tin, alternating between colours. Gently tap the tin on the bench to remove any large air pockets. Bake for about 1 hour or until a skewer inserted into the centre of the cake comes out clean. Leave the cake to cool in the tin for at least 30 minutes before turning out onto a wire rack to cool completely.

VANILLA BUTTERCREAM

110 g (3¾ oz) unsalted butter, softened
3 cups (420 g) icing (confectioners') sugar, sifted
¼ cup (60 ml) milk
1 teaspoon vanilla bean paste
Pink, red, violet, orange, blue, green and yellow gel food colouring

1. Using an electric mixer, beat the butter until very pale. Gradually add the icing sugar while beating on low speed. Add the milk and vanilla and beat on high speed until fluffy.
2. Take out half of the buttercream and divide it among seven bowls. Mix the colouring into each bowl until the desired shade is reached.

ASSEMBLY AND DECORATION

Mini craft pompoms
1 Ken doll with legs 'popped' off
Hot glue gun (optional)
Piping gel
Adhesive craft gems
Foil
Craft feathers in various colours
Sticky tape
Edible glitter

1. Using a long, thin knife, trim the cake so that it will sit level. Divide the cake into three even horizontal layers.

2. Working on a cake turntable or lazy Susan, secure the bottom layer of cake onto a cake board or large serving plate with a dollop of buttercream and then gently twist in place. Use an offset spatula to apply a generous layer of buttercream to the top of the cake, spreading it right to the edge.

3. Place the second cake layer on top and use the offset spatula to crumb coat the side of the cake with a thin layer of buttercream (see page 240). Repeat the layering process until the last cake layer is added. Carefully smooth the side until the desired finish is achieved. Chill the cake in the refrigerator for 20 minutes to firm.

4. Use an offset spatula to roughly apply a final rustic yet luscious-looking layer of buttercream all over the cake. Use a small offset spatula to apply the coloured buttercream in small dabs and strokes, cleaning the spatula in between each colour.

5. Using the picture on page 212 as a guide, stick the pompoms to the doll's head using a hot glue gun, piping gel or buttercream. Stick some adhesive gems across the doll's forehead. Cut strips of foil for the choker, wrist cuffs and belt. Trim the feathers to size. Attach the choker and feathered wrist cuffs to the doll using piping gel or sticky tape. Attach the feathers to the doll's back using sticky tape or a hot glue gun.

6. Brush the doll's torso with piping gel and decorate with edible glitter. Allow the glitter to dry before attaching the belt and carefully positioning the doll on the cake.

7. Wrap foil around one of the doll's legs to create a boot. Decorate the boot with adhesive gems. Remove a small wedge of cake (make sure you eat it!) and stick the leg into the cake. Finish with another feather to cover the join.

STORAGE

- This cake is best enjoyed on the day of decorating and can be refrigerated for up to 4 days. Serve it at room temperature.
- You can bake the cake a day ahead and store it at room temperature, tightly covered with plastic wrap. You can also refrigerate it for up to 2 days or freeze it for up to 2 months. Thaw overnight in the refrigerator before decorating.

Decorating Tips

- For the most intense buttercream colours, tint the buttercream the day before. This allows the colour to 'develop' overnight, leading to a richer colour. You can also gently heat the buttercream, which allows the food colouring to mix through more evenly and thoroughly.
- If you want to keep the doll's legs intact, wrap them in plastic wrap. You'll need to hollow out part of the cake to allow room for the legs.
- You can use any rainbow-coloured fluffy accessories instead of feathers and pompoms – just don't eat them!

Spoon the coloured batter into the Dolly Varden tin, alternating between the colours.

Secure the bottom layer of cake onto a cake board, then apply a generous layer of buttercream, followed by the second cake layer.

Crumb coat the bottom two cake layers, then spread another layer of buttercream over the top and add the final cake layer.

Use a small offset spatula to apply the coloured buttercream to the cake in dabs and strokes.

Clean the spatula each time you change to a different colour of buttercream so that the colours don't blend.

Continue applying the coloured buttercream all over the cake until you are happy with the result.

GREAT AUSSIE DREAM HOME

'The cost of living is rising!' 'House prices have surged!' 'Live with your parents till you're 42!' Owning a suburban house with picket fence on a quarter-acre block was once the ultimate expression of success, but the Great Australian Dream now seems about as attainable as a tan in Tasmania. This cake makes for a perfect house-warming gift for anyone who's switching rentals or has made it onto the property ladder. It's an exercise in Dream Home Design 101 because, after all, bakers are the great architects of the food world!

SERVES 40

VANILLA SPONGE CAKE

320 g (11¼ oz) unsalted butter, softened

2 cups (440 g) caster sugar

3 cups (480 g) self-raising flour, sifted

2 teaspoons vanilla extract

8 eggs, lightly whisked

⅓ cup (80 ml) hot water

1. Preheat the oven to 160°C (320°F) fan forced. Grease a 25 cm (10 inch) square cake tin and line the tin with baking paper.

2. Using an electric mixer, beat the butter and sugar until light, pale and creamy. Add 4 tablespoons of the flour, then gradually add the vanilla and eggs, beating well after each addition.

3. Gently fold in the remaining flour and the hot water.

4. Pour the batter into the tin. Bake for 50–60 minutes or until the centre of the cake springs back when lightly pressed. Leave in the tin for 30 minutes before carefully transferring to a wire rack to cool completely.

CHOCOLATE MUDCAKE

400 g (14 oz) unsalted butter, chopped

400 g (14 oz) good-quality dark chocolate, chopped

1¾ cups (395 g) caster sugar

1 cup (110 g) cocoa powder, sifted

1 cup (250 ml) hot water

2 tablespoons instant coffee powder

2 teaspoons vanilla extract

6 eggs, at room temperature

1½ cups (240 g) self-raising flour

1. Preheat the oven to 160°C (320°F) fan forced. Grease a 25 cm (10 inch) square cake tin and line the tin with baking paper.

2. Combine the butter, chocolate, sugar, cocoa, hot water, coffee and vanilla in a saucepan. Cook over low heat, whisking constantly, until smooth and well combined. Remove from the heat and set aside until lukewarm.

3. Using an electric mixer, whisk the eggs into the chocolate mixture until well combined. Sift the flour over the mixture and whisk until well combined.

4. Pour the batter into the tin. Bake for 1½ hours or until a skewer inserted into the centre of the cake comes out almost clean. (The centre will be sticky, but will come together once cooled.) Leave in the tin to cool completely, then cover the tin with plastic wrap and refrigerate for at least 1 hour.

DARK CHOCOLATE SWISS MERINGUE BUTTERCREAM

1½ cups (330 g) caster sugar
8 large egg whites
300 g (10½ oz) good-quality dark
 chocolate, chopped
2 cups (500 g) unsalted butter,
 softened
1 teaspoon vanilla extract

1. Put the sugar and egg whites in a heatproof glass bowl. Set the bowl over a pan of gently simmering water and whisk until the sugar has dissolved and the mixture is slightly warm to the touch. Remove from the heat.

2. Using an electric mixer fitted with the whisk attachment, beat on high speed until the mixture has formed stiff and glossy peaks (about 10–15 minutes).

3. Meanwhile, melt the chocolate using either the microwave or double-boiler method (see page 245). Remove from the heat and keep warm.

4. Add the butter to the meringue in three batches, beating until incorporated after each addition. (Don't be alarmed if it appears curdled – it will become light and fluffy with continued whipping, I promise!) Beat in the chocolate. Add the vanilla and beat until fluffy, then beat on low speed to eliminate air bubbles. Cover the bowl with plastic wrap and set aside in a cool place until needed.

VANILLA BEAN SWISS MERINGUE BUTTERCREAM

1½ cups (330 g) caster sugar
8 large egg whites
2 cups (500 g) unsalted butter,
 softened
1 teaspoon vanilla bean paste or
 vanilla extract
Turquoise gel food colouring

1. Put the sugar and egg whites in a heatproof glass bowl. Set the bowl over a pan of gently simmering water and whisk until the sugar has dissolved and the mixture is slightly warm to the touch. Remove from the heat.

2. Using an electric mixer fitted with the whisk attachment, beat on high speed until the mixture has formed stiff and glossy peaks (about 10–15 minutes).

3. Add the butter in three batches, beating until incorporated after each addition. Add the vanilla and beat until fluffy.

4. Tint the buttercream turquoise, then beat on low speed to eliminate air bubbles, if needed. Cover the bowl with plastic wrap and set aside in a cool place until needed.

ASSEMBLY AND DECORATION

30 liquorice allsorts
30 square wafer biscuits
1 large round gummy jelly, halved
4 triangular gummy jellies, halved
50 g (1¾ oz) white chocolate,
    melted
25 white chocolate biscuit fingers,
    halved
25 milk chocolate biscuit fingers,
    halved
6 round chocolate-coated biscuits
Black liquorice rope
Edible gold lustre dust
8 jersey caramels
10 gummy spearmint leaves
6 gummy fruits
1 rainbow fruit Roll-Ups
1 cup (85 g) desiccated coconut
Green food colouring
25 sugar flower decorations

1. Turn the mudcake out of the tin. Use a long, thin knife to level the top of the mudcake and the sponge cake. Divide each cake into two horizontal layers.

2. Referring to the pictures on pages 222 to 223, secure the bottom layer of mudcake onto a large cake board with a dollop of chocolate buttercream (you may need to use a large spatula to lift the cake to prevent it from splitting). Use an offset spatula to cover the top of the cake with a 1 cm (½ inch) layer of chocolate buttercream, spreading it right to the edge.

3. Place a layer of sponge cake on top of the mudcake and gently press down to secure. Top with chocolate buttercream and repeat the layering process with the remaining cake layers, alternating between mudcake and sponge cake. Chill in the refrigerator for at least 30 minutes or until firm.

4. Use a long, thin knife to cut off the back third of the layered cake and cut this section into two triangular pieces. Spread a layer of buttercream on top of the cake, then carefully position the triangular cake pieces to form the sloped roof, securing them with more buttercream. Trim away any excess. Return the cake to the refrigerator for 15 minutes.

5. Using an offset spatula and a cake scraper, gently crumb coat the entire cake with a thin layer of turquoise buttercream (see page 240). Carefully smooth the side until the desired finish is achieved. Chill in the refrigerator for 10–15 minutes.

6. Apply a final generous layer of turquoise buttercream all over the chilled cake. Use the cake scraper to smooth the sides and top (see page 241) – or you may choose a more rustic finish.

7. Using the picture on page 217 as a guide, use sliced liquorice allsorts to form the windows and door. (Reserve four whole liquorice allsorts for the chimney.) Decorate the roof of the house by gently placing the wafer biscuits on top. Stick the halved gummy jellies above the door to create a sun feature.

8. Create a picket fence by sticking the halved chocolate finger biscuits to the board using the melted chocolate.

9. Make the water tank by sticking the round chocolate biscuits together with the melted chocolate. Cut the liquorice rope to size and wrap it around the biscuit stack, securing it with melted chocolate, if needed. Lightly dust the liquorice with lustre dust to create a corrugated iron effect. Gently position the water tank next to the house.

10. Make the chimney by sticking the jersey caramels and whole liquorice allsorts together using the melted chocolate. Use a sharp knife to cut a diagonal slice from the bottom of the chimney so that it sits upright on the roof. Secure the chimney to the roof using melted chocolate.

STORAGE

- This cake is best enjoyed at room temperature. It can be refrigerated for up to 5 days. Note that the wafer biscuits may soften once refrigerated.

- You can bake the sponge cake 2 days in advance and the mudcake 4 days in advance. Tightly cover with plastic wrap and store at room temperature or in the refrigerator, or freeze for up to 2 months. Thaw the cakes overnight in the refrigerator before using.

- Refrigerate the chocolate and vanilla buttercream in separate airtight containers for up to 10 days or freeze them for up to 2 months. Thaw overnight in the refrigerator, then bring to room temperature before using. Beat with an electric mixer on low speed until smooth.

11. Arrange the gummy spearmint leaves and fruits around the base of the cake to form the garden. Cut the fruit Roll-Ups to size and place in front of the door to create the path.

12. Put the coconut in a resealable plastic bag and add a few drops of green colouring. Seal the bag, then shake the bag and massage the coconut until it reaches the desired shade. Spoon around the house to create the lawn.

13. Tint the remaining turquoise buttercream with green food colouring and spoon it into a piping bag fitted with a grass tip or multi-opening tip. Pipe tufts of 'grass' around the base of the house and around the fence line. Decorate with the sugar flowers. Once the edible landscaping is done, invite your friends around for a house warming!

Decorating Tip

- I used Arnott's Tina Wafer biscuits to decorate the roof, and Cadbury Breakaway biscuits to create the water tank.

Secure the bottom layer of mudcake onto a large cake board and cover it with a layer of chocolate buttercream.

You may need to use a large spatula or cake lifter to lift the cake layers to prevent them from splitting.

Continue layering the cakes and buttercream, alternating between mudcake and sponge cake.

Carefully lift up the first layered cake triangle in one piece and place it on top of the buttercream-covered cake.

Position the first layered cake triangle on top of the cake, lining it up with the front of the cake.

Add the second layered cake triangle, removing any excess cake, and gently press the layers together.

Next, use the spatula to crumb coat the entire cake with a rough layer of turquoise buttercream.

Once you have added the final layer of turquoise buttercream, use a cake scraper to smooth the sides and top of the cake.

MAD MAX ROAD WARRIOR CAKE

Set in a not-too-distant dystopian future, when man's most precious resource, cake flour, has been depleted and the world plunged into war, famine and financial chaos... At least that's how I remember the movie. Released in 1979 by Australian director George Miller, *Mad Max* took the world by dust storm. In the same way that the film has attracted a cult following, its monstrously modified vehicles are celebrity figures in the auto-mechanic world. If you haven't yet forayed into the world of car cakes, why not start with the most hectic of them all? 'I'm just here for the gasoline'... actually, I think he meant cake.

SERVES 16—20

CHOCOLATE MUDCAKE

600 g (1 lb 5 oz) unsalted butter, chopped
600 g (1 lb 5 oz) good-quality dark chocolate, chopped
600 g (1 lb 5 oz) caster sugar
1½ cups (165 g) cocoa powder, sifted
1½ cups (375 ml) hot water
½ cup (35 g) instant coffee powder
3 teaspoons vanilla extract
8 large eggs, at room temperature
2¼ cups (360 g) self-raising flour

1. Preheat the oven to 160°C (320°F) fan forced. Grease a 25 cm (10 inch) square cake tin and line the tin with baking paper.

2. Combine the butter, chocolate, sugar, cocoa, hot water, coffee and vanilla in a saucepan. Cook over low heat, whisking constantly, until smooth and well combined. Remove from the heat and set aside until lukewarm.

3. Using an electric mixer, whisk the eggs into the chocolate mixture until well combined. Sift the flour over the mixture and whisk until well combined.

4. Pour the batter into the tin. Bake for 1½ hours or until a skewer inserted into the centre of the cake comes out almost clean. (The centre will be sticky, but will come together once cooled.) Leave in the tin to cool completely, then cover the tin with plastic wrap and refrigerate for at least 1 hour.

BLACK ESPRESSO CHOCOLATE GANACHE

400 ml (14 fl oz) single (pure) cream
800 g (1 lb 12 oz) good-quality dark chocolate, chopped
¼ cup (20 g) instant coffee powder
Black gel food colouring or powder

1. Pour the cream into a small saucepan and bring to a rolling boil (there should be bubbles all over the surface, not just around the edge). Remove from the heat and add the chocolate, stirring until there are no lumps. Add the coffee powder and stir until dissolved.

2. Tint the ganache with a small amount of black colouring, keeping in mind that it will appear one to two shades richer once set.

3. Set the ganache aside overnight at room temperature to thicken.

ASSEMBLY AND DECORATION

35 cm (14 inch) square silver cake
  board or serving platter covered
  in silver or grey vinyl adhesive
  paper
200 g (7 oz) black fondant
Cornflour, for rolling
Black liquorice rope
2 liquorice twists
½ large Cadbury Boost bar,
  cut in half
Edible silver and gold paint

1. Photocopy the template opposite, enlarging it by 150%, then carefully cut out the template.

2. Use a long, thin knife to divide the cake horizontally into two even layers.

3. Use an offset spatula to apply a generous layer of chocolate ganache to the top of the bottom cake layer, spreading it right to the edges. Place the second cake layer on top.

4. Using the template and the pictures on page 228 as a guide, carve the cake into the car shape. (Save the offcuts to eat later!)

5. Use an offset spatula to apply a layer of chocolate ganache all over the cake. Use a small cake scraper to smooth the ganache until the desired finish is achieved. Chill the cake in the refrigerator for 30–60 minutes.

6. To make the wheels, roll out the black fondant on a board dusted with cornflour until about 1 cm (½ inch) thick. Use a 5 cm (2 inch) round cookie cutter to cut out four wheels. Set aside until firm and dry.

7. Roll out the fondant into strips about 1–2 mm (¹⁄₁₆ inch) thick and slice to create two spoilers and two headlights for the car. Cut thinner strips for the windscreen wipers. Set aside to dry.

8. Cut two 2.5 cm (1 inch) pieces of liquorice rope to create the pipes in front of the back wheels. Paint the liquorice pieces, liquorice twists and chocolate bar half with silver edible paint. Add the silver details on the fondant wheels, headlights and spoilers. Use gold paint to add more depth and detail.

9. Paint the large silver details onto the cake, such as the windows and windscreen. Position the windscreen wipers on top. Use a small paint brush to paint the finer details, such as the door and bonnet lines.

10. Position the silver parts in place on the car.

Decorating Tips

- You can prepare the ganache using the microwave. Combine the chocolate and cream in a microwave-safe bowl and microwave on High in 1-minute intervals, stirring for 2 minutes in between, until there are no lumps. I use a stick blender to stir the cream and melted chocolate together as it's much quicker and easier to ensure an even consistency.

- Speed up the cooling time for the ganache by placing it in the refrigerator or freezer and stirring every 20–30 minutes until the desired consistency is reached.

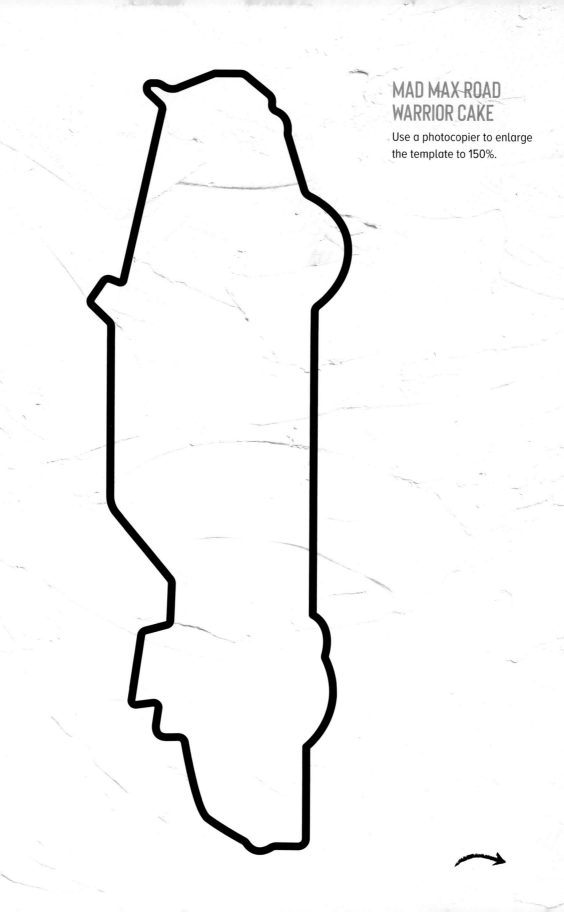

MAD MAX ROAD WARRIOR CAKE

Use a photocopier to enlarge
the template to 150%.

Using a long, thin knife, cut the chocolate mudcake horizontally into two even layers.

Use the knife to level the top of the cake, then brush away any excess cake crumbs.

Use an offset spatula to apply a thick layer of the chocolate ganache to the top of the bottom cake layer.

Carefully add the second cake layer and press gently to help the layers stick together.

Cut the cake in half, then arrange the two cake halves at right angles and use a little ganache to attach the template to the side.

Carve the cake into the car shape, using a long, straight knife to cut into the cake and remove the pieces.

THE BOTANIC GARDENS OF CAKE

We love a good botanic garden (particularly if we can have an Aussie picnic in it).
This striking number captures the spirit of our lively nationwide collection of gardens,
and will bring your baking prowess into full bloom. It would make a stunning celebration cake
for a special birthday or small wedding. Botanic gardens educate us all about our natural flora,
biodiversity and plant conservation. So many reasons to celebrate! If you're not into growing
edible flower varieties in a windowbox or in your backyard, you'll find them at local farmers'
markets and specialty grocers. Or hop online to order them.

SERVES 30—35

CHOCOLATE SPONGE CAKE

20 CM (8 INCH) CAKE
350 g (12 oz) unsalted butter, softened
350 g (12 oz) caster sugar
7 eggs, at room temperature
350 g (12 oz) self-raising flour
⅔ cup (75 g) cocoa powder

13 CM (5 INCH) CAKE
140 g (5 oz) unsalted butter, softened
140 g (5 oz) caster sugar
3 eggs, at room temperature
140 g (5 oz) self-raising flour
¼ cup (30 g) cocoa powder

1. Preheat the oven to 160°C (320°F) fan forced. Lightly grease three 20 cm (8 inch) cake layer tins and three 13 cm (5 inch) cake layer tins. Line the cake tins with baking paper, with the paper extending 7.5 cm (3 inches) above the top of the tin to prevent the cakes from spilling over. Prepare and bake the cakes one at a time so that they rise evenly.

2. To prepare the layers for the 20 cm cake tier, use an electric mixer to beat the butter and sugar until light and fluffy. Add the eggs, one at a time, and beat until fluffy.

3. Fold in the flour and cocoa until combined.

4. Divide the batter evenly among the cake tins and level the surface using a spatula or the back of a spoon. Bake for 25–30 minutes or until the tops of the cakes spring back when gently pressed. Cool in the tins for 10 minutes and then carefully turn the cakes out onto a wire rack to cool completely. Cover with plastic wrap and set aside until needed.

5. Prepare the layers for the 13 cm cake tier using the same method and reducing the cooking time to 20–25 minutes.

RASPBERRY CREAM CHEESE FROSTING

200 g (7 oz) unsalted butter,
   softened
1 kg (2 lb 4 oz) cream cheese,
   softened
2 teaspoons vanilla bean paste
3 teaspoons lemon juice
1 tablespoon single (pure) cream
3 cups (420 g) icing (confectioners')
   sugar
40 g (1¼ oz) freeze-dried raspberry
   powder (see tips)
Pink gel food colouring

1. Using an electric mixer, beat the butter on medium speed until creamy. Add the cream cheese, vanilla and lemon juice and beat until creamy. Gradually increase the speed to high and continue beating until light and fluffy.

2. Add the cream and beat until light and fluffy. Gradually sift in the icing sugar, beating on low speed until well combined. Add the raspberry powder and mix until blended, then increase the speed to high and beat until well combined and smooth. While beating, add the pink food colouring until the desired shade is reached.

3. Chill the frosting in the refrigerator for about 1 hour or until it has firmed to a more workable consistency for piping onto the cake layers.

ASSEMBLY AND DECORATION

1 cup (320 g) raspberry jam,
   warmed
4 wooden cake dowels or sturdy
   plastic straws
10 cm (4 inch) round cardboard
   cake stacking board
Edible fresh flowers

1. Use a pastry brush to brush the outside edges and top of each cake layer with the warmed jam.

2. Working on a cake turntable or lazy Susan, secure the bottom layer of the large cake onto a cake stand, plate or cake board with a dollop of frosting and then gently twist in place. Fill a piping bag fitted with a star nozzle with the frosting. Starting from the outside edge, pipe the frosting onto the cake layer until completely covered.

3. Gently place the second cake layer on top and continue layering until you add the last layer of the large cake. If the filling is squeezing out between the layers, or if the cake feels unsteady (this will happen in warmer kitchens), refrigerate the cake until the filling has set before continuing.

4. Insert one of the cake dowels about 2.5 cm (1 inch) from the centre of the cake. Mark the height of the cake with your thumb, remove the dowel and mark the height with a pen. Cut the dowel with scissors or a serrated knife and use it as a guide when cutting the remaining dowels. Insert the dowels into the cake, 2.5 cm (1 inch) from the centre and evenly spaced.

5. Pipe a small dollop of frosting on top of the cake and press the cardboard circle in place. Pipe another small dollop of frosting onto the cardboard and press the bottom layer of the small cake in place.

6. Pipe a layer of frosting to cover the cake layer, then add the remaining cake layers, piping a layer of frosting in between each. Decorate the top of the large and small cakes with piped frosting.

7. Adorn the cake with a glorious array of fresh edible flowers.

Decorating Tips

- You can also bake the cakes in one deep 20 cm (8 inch) cake tin and one deep 13 cm (5 inch) cake tin. Bake the large cake for 50–60 minutes and the small cake for 40–50 minutes. Once completely cooled, use a long, thin knife to divide each cake into three even layers.
- Replace the raspberry powder with ½ cup (125 ml) puréed raspberries or ½ cup (160 g) 100% fruit raspberry jam if you like.
- I used raspberry jam to fill the cake, but you can use any flavour you like.

STORAGE

- This cake is best enjoyed on the day of decorating but it can be refrigerated for up to 4 days. The flowers will begin to wilt after 2 days.
- You can bake the cakes up to 2 days ahead and store them in an airtight container or covered in plastic wrap in the refrigerator, or freeze them for up to 1 month. Thaw them in the refrigerator before decorating.
- The frosting can be prepared up to 5 days ahead and refrigerated in an airtight container, or frozen for up to 1 month. Thaw it in the refrigerator overnight, then gently reheat in the microwave in 20-second bursts, stirring in between.

CHAPTER 4

BASICS

This is where you'll find all the tricks of the trade. Discover how to get organised and bake like a boss. Make your cakes and fillings in advance and store them to spread the working load. Learn fool-proof techniques for cutting, filling, icing and layering your cakes.

TOOLS OF THE TRADE

My best advice for home baking success is to be well-equipped. In addition to basic kitchen utensils, mixing bowls and appliances, the following tools and equipment will make the wonderful process of creating and baking easier and more enjoyable:

- offset metal spatulas in varying sizes
- cake scrapers of varying heights
- a candy thermometer
- a long, thin knife or a cake leveller for slicing cakes into layers
- a stable and smooth-spinning cake turntable or lazy Susan (this will save both your time and sanity when it comes to frosting a cake!)
- basic piping tips and piping bags (reusable or disposable – biodegradable if possible)
- gel food colouring (for colouring cakes, meringue, buttercream, fondant and ganache)
- oil-based or powdered food colouring (for colouring chocolate).

Make sure you have a happy assortment of sprinkles and candies. Combine different types to make your very own fun mixture. Look in confectionery stores, cake decorating stores and online for different and unusual sprinkles and lollies.

The most important tool of all is the oven. As every oven is slightly different, an oven thermometer may be a good investment to ensure your oven is calibrated to the correct temperature – especially if there are 'hot spots' in the oven, or if it loses heat quickly when the door is opened. The thermometer will guide you in adjusting the temperature or baking times accordingly. Check the manufacturer's instructions for best results, and get to know and understand your oven's nuances through lots of good baking practice!

It's important to use accurate scales, measuring spoons, cups and jugs. I use Australian standard metric measurements, but have also included imperial conversions in the recipes. Note that 1 Australian tablespoon is equal to 20 ml, whereas 1 imperial tablespoon is equal to 15 ml. If you are using an imperial tablespoon, adjust your measurements accordingly.

CUTTING, FILLING AND FROSTING

When you're making a layered cake, the first step is to cut the cake into layers (unless, of course, you've baked the cake in separate layers). The second step is to layer the cake with the filling. Once you've added the final cake layer, check that your cake is straight and level — feel free to push and manipulate the cake layers so that they are as close to straight as possible.

Next it's time to crumb coat the cake with a thin layer of frosting, trapping the crumbs inside so that the final coat of frosting is clean and smooth. Last of all, the final layer of frosting is applied and smoothed until you're happy with the finish — whether that's a completely smooth look or a more rustic style.

CUTTING THE CAKE INTO LAYERS

Place the cake on a cake turntable and use a long, thin knife or cake leveller to divide the cake into two or three even layers.

Secure the bottom layer of cake onto a cake board with a dollop of buttercream, then check that the top is level.

FILLING THE CAKE: BASIC LAYERING

Cover the cake layer with a thin layer of lemon curd or jam, if using, then add a generous portion of buttercream.

Using an offset spatula, spread the buttercream right to the edge of the cake.

FILLING THE CAKE: THE 'DAM' METHOD

Alternatively, use the 'dam' method: with a piping bag, pipe a ring of buttercream around the edge of the cake layer.

Fill the buttercream 'dam' with the filling of your choice, then add the next layer of cake and continue filling and layering.

CRUMB COATING THE CAKE

Using an offset spatula, fill in any gaps between the layers with frosting, then add several dollops of frosting towards the base of the cake and spread it up the side and over the top of the cake.

The goal is to create a thin layer of frosting that completely coats the cake – it doesn't need to be perfectly smooth. Once completed, chill the cake in the fridge for 10–20 minutes.

ADDING THE FINAL LAYER OF FROSTING

Apply the frosting as for the crumb coat, starting with several dollops of frosting around the base, then continue adding and spreading the frosting until there is an even layer all over. Make sure there is enough buttercream to make a substantial top layer – it still doesn't need to be completely smooth at this stage, just relatively even.

SMOOTHING THE SIDE AND TOP

Hold a cake scraper parallel to the cake and rotate the turntable with your free hand, cleaning the cake scraper after every few spins. Repeat until smooth, filling in any gaps with extra frosting.

Using the edge of an offset spatula, gently pull the 'lip' of excess frosting towards the centre of the cake and work around the top of the cake, cleaning the spatula with every swipe.

TIP: To transfer your cake to a cake stand or serving plate (either from a turntable or from a cake board), gently run a clean offset spatula all around the base of the cake to release it, then carefully slide the spatula underneath the cake and lift. You can even use a large barbecue spatula to help with this. I highly recommend that you chill the cake until firm in the fridge or freezer before moving it – it makes the whole process much easier, and helps prevent blemishes appearing on the buttercream.

HOW TO STACK
A TIERED CAKE

Making a simple tiered cake need not be daunting! The most important thing to remember when constructing a tiered (also known as stacked) cake is: SUPPORT. The cake needs adequate support to ensure that it won't sink into a bulging heap. There are different kinds of dowels that can be used to support a cake, such as wooden cake dowels, hollow plastic dowels, sturdy plastic straws and even wooden skewers. Whatever you choose, it needs to be food-safe.

My personal preference when building a tiered cake is to use wooden cake dowels. They can be found in cake decorating stores and are sturdy yet inexpensive. The tiered cake sizes I usually make are 23 cm (9 inches), 18 cm (7 inches) and 13 cm (5 inches). Of course, you can use different sizes according to the cake requirements — and how much you are physically able to lift!

Mark the height of the dowels and trim them using a pair of dog nail clippers (I have a pair just for cutting cake dowels), small branch pruners or dowel cutters.

Insert the four trimmed dowels into the cake, well inside where the next cake tier will sit, and use a spare cake dowel to push them right down into the cake.

Add the cake dowels to the second cake tier, then carefully lift the second tier (including the cardboard cake circle) on top of the first tier using a metal spatula or a cake lifter.

Use a large offset spatula to help gently slide the second cake tier off the cake lifter and into position in the centre of the first cake tier.

To make sure the tiers won't slide off, sharpen one end of a long wooden dowel, slightly shorter than the cake, with a clean pencil sharpener and drive the dowel down through all the cake layers.

Mask the hole created on top of the cake, as well as any other gaps or blemishes between the tiers, with an offset spatula and a little left-over frosting. Finish decorating the cake as desired.

A WORD ON CHOCOLATE

Over many years of enthusiastic chocolate-eating and chocolate-handling, I've discovered that the realm of chocolate is a fascinating and multi-faceted discipline of its own. While I have undertaken several courses on chocolate in an attempt to properly educate myself, I can't claim to have a firm grasp on this luxury ingredient. However, I have learned the basics for home baking.

There are two types of chocolate you're likely to come across: couverture chocolate and compound chocolate.

Couverture chocolate refers to chocolate that contains more than 31% cocoa butter. Cocoa butter is the natural fat found in cocoa beans; it's what allows couverture chocolate to contract and it provides a glossy sheen. I think the taste and smooth mouth feel of couverture chocolate are divine!

Cocoa butter is the component in couverture chocolate that must be tempered (also known more often these days as 'crystallised'). Untempered chocolate can have a gritty texture and may appear discoloured. Also, it doesn't set completely at room temperature, which can be frustrating when you're unknowingly working with untempered chocolate at home.

Compound chocolate is a different type of chocolate altogether and it is most widely available. It is cheaper, as most (if not all) of the cocoa butter has been removed and replaced with other ingredients like hydrogenated vegetable fats and milk powders. It has a much higher melting point than couverture chocolate and does not need to be tempered. Compound chocolate is sometimes sold as decorators' chocolate or chocolate melts.

While I prefer the taste of couverture chocolate, I do use compound chocolate in my cakes and desserts when the chocolate isn't the 'main player'. It's quick and easy to use when I'm making no-fuss chocolate decorations.

Whatever chocolate you use, it's important to store it at room temperature, but not above 24°C (75.2°F). It should be protected from natural light and moisture.

TEMPERING AND MELTING CHOCOLATE

Here are some standard methods for tempering couverture chocolate or melting chocolate at home.

TEMPERING COUVERTURE CHOCOLATE

1. This is known as the 'seeding' method. Before you begin, make sure you have a trusted candy thermometer on hand.

2. Melt two-thirds of the chocolate in a clean, dry, heatproof bowl over a saucepan of just simmering water (the water should not touch the base of the bowl), gently stirring with a silicone spatula. When the chocolate reaches 40–45°C (104–113°F) on the thermometer, remove the bowl from the saucepan.

3. Add the remaining chocolate to the bowl. Stir until the temperature drops to 27°C (80.6°F) and all the chocolate has melted. Return the bowl to the pan of simmering water and heat until it reaches 29–30°C (84.2–86°F) for milk and white chocolate, or 31–32°C (87.8–89.6°F) for dark chocolate. Use immediately.

MELTING CHOCOLATE

Double-boiler method: Put the chocolate in a clean, dry, heatproof bowl over a saucepan of just simmering water (the water should not touch the base of the bowl). Gently stir with a silicone spatula until melted. Use immediately.

Microwave method: Put the chocolate in a clean, dry, heatproof bowl and microwave at 50% power, stirring intermittently with a rubber spatula until melted.

MAKE IT YOURSELF...

I think the satisfaction earned from making something utterly delicious from scratch is worth the effort. Plus, you'll know exactly what's going into your food and the mouths of your loved ones. An added benefit is that you can tailor everything to suit your tastes – I never find store-bought lemon curd or salted caramel quite as decadent as the versions I make myself.

EASY-PEASY LEMON CURD

I spread lemon curd on toast, stir it through yoghurt, dollop it on pancakes and use it to fill layered cakes. It can be refrigerated for up to 1 week.

MAKES 3 CUPS (750 ML)

2 eggs
6 egg yolks
Grated zest of 2 lemons
1 cup (250 ml) strained fresh lemon juice
1 cup (220 g) caster sugar
¾ cup (180 g) unsalted butter, chopped

1. Whisk the eggs and the yolks in a small non-reactive saucepan until combined. Whisk in the lemon zest, juice and sugar. Add the butter.

2. Place the pan over medium heat and whisk, scraping the bottom and side of the pan, until the butter is melted and the mixture is thickened and beginning to simmer around the edge. Continue whisking for a further 10 seconds. Remove the pan from the heat.

3. Scrape the lemon curd into a strainer set over a bowl to remove the lemon zest, if you wish. Chill in the refrigerator before using.

SALTED CARAMEL

Refrigerate the salted caramel in an airtight container for up to 2 weeks, or freeze for up to 2 months.

MAKES 3 CUPS (750 ML)

2 cups (440 g) caster sugar
¾ cup (180 g) unsalted butter, chopped
1 cup (250 ml) single (pure) cream or thick (double) cream
2 teaspoons salt

1. Heat the sugar in a saucepan over medium heat, stirring constantly with a heatproof silicone spatula or wooden spoon. The sugar will form clumps and eventually melt into a thick, amber-coloured liquid.

2. As soon as the sugar is completely melted, carefully add the butter – the mixture will bubble rapidly when the butter is added. Stir the butter into the caramel until it is completely melted, about 2–3 minutes.

3. Continue stirring as you very slowly drizzle in the cream. (Because the cream is colder than the caramel, the mixture will rapidly bubble and splatter when added.) Allow the mixture to boil for 1 minute – it will rise in the pan as it boils.

4. Remove the pan from the heat and stir in the salt, to taste. Allow to cool completely before using. For a thinner consistency, stir in more cream.

MARSHMALLOW FONDANT

Home-made marshmallow fondant is a delicious fondant alternative that can be used to decorate cakes and cupcakes. You can also flavour it to suit your taste (I like vanilla and coconut) and tint it with gel food colouring. I highly recommend making the fondant at least 24 hours before you need it. Resting the fondant ensures a smoother and more workable texture. In my experience, fondant made on the same day will more than likely be too soft and tear easily. Don't do it to yourself!

MAKES 1.5 KG (3 LB 5 OZ)

500 g (1 lb 2 oz) white marshmallows
2 tablespoons water
Flavouring (optional)
Gel food colouring (optional)
1 kg (2 lb 4 oz) icing (confectioners') sugar, sifted

1. Put the marshmallows and water in a large microwave-safe bowl. Microwave on High for 1–2 minutes or until the marshmallows are puffed up and starting to melt. Carefully stir until smooth.

2. Add a drop of flavouring and/or colouring (if using). Stir until well combined.

3. Using a spoon or spatula, slowly mix in the icing sugar, reserving 1 cup (140 g) for kneading. Mix until you have a very stiff dough.

4. Transfer the icing to a clean surface that has been well-dusted with icing sugar. Knead until the fondant is smooth and no longer sticky to the touch (about 5–10 minutes).

5. Roll the fondant into a ball and tightly wrap in plastic wrap. Place in the refrigerator overnight.

6. Bring the fondant to room temperature before using. Roll it out on a clean surface that has been well-dusted with icing sugar. Store any left-over fondant in the refrigerator to prevent mould growth.

TIPS

- If you plan on colouring your fondant pink, use pink marshmallows to make the fondant instead of white.

- Always work on a thoroughly clean surface, and cover the surface and your hands with sifted icing sugar. You can also grease your hands with vegetable shortening to prevent them from sticking to the fondant.

- Avoid making marshmallow fondant in dark colours such as black, navy blue or bright red – it's difficult to achieve these shades without going through LOADS of food colouring. To save the drama, I would recommend using store-bought coloured fondant.

- Marshmallow fondant can be stored at room temperature for 1–2 days or refrigerated for up to 10 days.

STORAGE TIPS

When you're making a cake for a big occasion, it's useful to be able to bake the cake and/or prepare the frosting a few days in advance. Not only does this leave you more time to decorate the cake on the big day, it also allows time for you to start again in the event of a baking disaster — and I have certainly had my share of those!

It's important to note that cakes containing cream cheese frosting or buttercream are best brought to room temperature before serving — there's nothing pleasant about eating a mouthful of solid cold buttercream!

CAKES

Most cakes can be baked a few days in advance. Once the cake is completely cool, tightly wrap it in plastic wrap before storing as indicated below.

Sponge cake: Bake up to 2 days in advance and store at room temperature or in the refrigerator.

Mudcake: Bake up to 4 days in advance and store at room temperature or in the refrigerator.

Choc-heaven cake: Bake up to 3 days in advance and store in the refrigerator.

Dark chocolate sea salt cake: Bake up to 1–2 days in advance and store at room temperature.

Violet velvet cake/Red velvet cake: Bake up to 1 day in advance and store at room temperature.

FREEZING CAKES

All of the cakes listed above can be frozen for up to 2 months (mudcakes can be frozen for up to 3 months). Once the cake is completely cool, tightly wrap the whole cake (or wrap each individual layer, if it's a layered cake) in two layers of plastic wrap and then place in an airtight container or freezer bag. Thaw the cake overnight in the refrigerator before decorating.

FROSTINGS, TOPPINGS AND FILLINGS

Most frostings, toppings and fillings are suitable to prepare in advance and store in an airtight container in the refrigerator or freezer. Thaw frozen buttercream and cream cheese frosting overnight in the refrigerator, then bring to room temperature (gently reheat in the microwave in 20-second bursts if needed). Beat buttercream and cream cheese frosting with an electric mixer on low speed until smooth before applying to your cake.

Buttercream: Refrigerate for up to 10 days or freeze for up to 2 months.

Swiss meringue buttercream: Refrigerate for up to 10 days or freeze for up to 2 months.

Cream cheese frosting: Refrigerate for up to 5 days or freeze for up to 1 month.

Ganache: Refrigerate for 5–7 days or freeze for up to 1 month. (Cover the surface with plastic wrap before storing.)

INDEX

ACKNOWLEDGEMENTS

As extraordinary as my little dog Pluto thinks I am, the creation of this cookbook was not a one-cake-lady effort. In reality, this project has been made possible due to the brilliance of MANY enthusiastic cake ladies — and a bunch of clever cake-loving men too. I'll forever owe the following folk my thanks, and maybe even a few birthday cakes here and there!

The passionate team at Murdoch Books have lovingly held my mixing bowl throughout this entire fun-filled process, and I am extremely grateful for not only their impressive brains but for their encouragement and (sometimes blind) faith in my ideas. It's not easy to envisage a koala cake in full Dame Edna get-up!

To our Publisher-in-Chief, Jane Morrow, thank you for being one of these galvanising people who have supported me from the very beginning of my new career. It's been a dream come true finally working alongside you, and I'm so grateful our beloved cookbook idea has come ALIVE!

Three cheers to our Creative Manager, Megan Pigott, for your vision and humour. Oh, and for better or for worse, we have Megan to thank for those scantily clad Budgie Smuggler cupcakes!

I owe our Managing Editor and wordsmith extraordinaire, Jane Price, many delicious delicacies for injecting the passages of this book with so much pizazz. When the puns don't write themselves, it's because they haven't met Jane Price.

Big thank you to Justine Harding for meticulously combing through each recipe and gilding them in gold with her supreme kitchen know-how. You have played such a valuable role in the user-friendliness and success of this book.

One wonderful name to remember is Emma Knowles — our talented Stylist, magic-maker and pavlova-whisperer. Emma, you are the facilitator of dreams! When split buttercream hits the fan, you know who's got the courage to whip it back into place.

Behind every great cake recipe is an equally great cake photo, and these gorgeous pages wouldn't be shining so brightly without the talents of Jeremy Simons, our Photographer and overlord of light. Thank you for your patience while Emma and I were 'dressing the talent' (and eating the offcuts!).

I'd like to blow another kiss to my brand spankin' new husband, Simon (Esjay) James. You've been my best savoury-toothed friend for over 8 years now, and I'm extremely excited to have you endure more cake talk for the rest of our snack-tastic lives. The next pub meal is my shout!

To my loving parents, my dear family, and my beautifully diverse friends, I'm so lucky to be a part of such a vibrant community of people.

Lastly (but not at all leastly!), I am hugely grateful to all of you beaut' readers and my new cake-loving mates for supporting me in the creation of my second cookbook. You are keeping this ridiculous dream of living my best 'Cake Life' alive. I owe you all the heartfelt hugs and high-fives in the world! *Bake Australia Great* is for anyone whose encouragement, friendship and kindness has allowed me to kick some major home-baking goals within the golden shores of this beautiful country. Cheers for inviting this cookbook to the party!

Kat xo

Published in 2019 by Murdoch Books, an imprint of Allen & Unwin

Murdoch Books Australia
83 Alexander Street, Crows Nest NSW 2065
Phone: +61 (0)2 8425 0100
murdochbooks.com.au
info@murdochbooks.com.au

Murdoch Books UK
Ormond House, 26—27 Boswell Street,
London, WC1N 3JZ
Phone: +44 (0) 20 8785 5995
murdochbooks.co.uk
info@murdochbooks.co.uk

For corporate orders & custom publishing contact our business development
team at salesenquiries@murdochbooks.com.au

Publisher: Jane Morrow
Creative Manager: Megan Pigott
Editorial Manager: Jane Price
Editor: Justine Harding
Cover and concept designer: Kirby Armstrong
Designers: Susanne Geppert and Megan Pigott
Photographer: Jeremy Simons
Stylist: Emma Knowles
Production Director: Lou Playfair

Text © Katherine Sabbath 2019
Design © Murdoch Books 2019
Photography © Jeremy Simons 2019

ISBN 978 1 76063 778 1 Australia
ISBN 978 1 91163 224 5 UK

A cataloguing-in-publication entry is available
from the catalogue of the National Library of
Australia at nla.gov.au

A catalogue record for this book is available from the British Library

Colour reproduction by Splitting Image Colour Studio Pty Ltd, Clayton, Victoria
Printed by C&C Offset Printing Co Ltd, China

TABLESPOON MEASURES: We have used Australian 20 ml (4 teaspoon) tablespoon measures.
If you are using a smaller European 15 ml (3 teaspoon) tablespoon, add an extra teaspoon
of the ingredient for each tablespoon specified.

IMPORTANT: Those who might be at risk from the effects of salmonella poisoning (the elderly,
pregnant women, young children and those suffering from immune deficiency diseases) should
consult their doctor with any concerns about eating raw eggs.

The paper in this book is FSC® certified.
FSC® promotes environmentally responsible,
socially beneficial and economically viable
management of the world's forests.

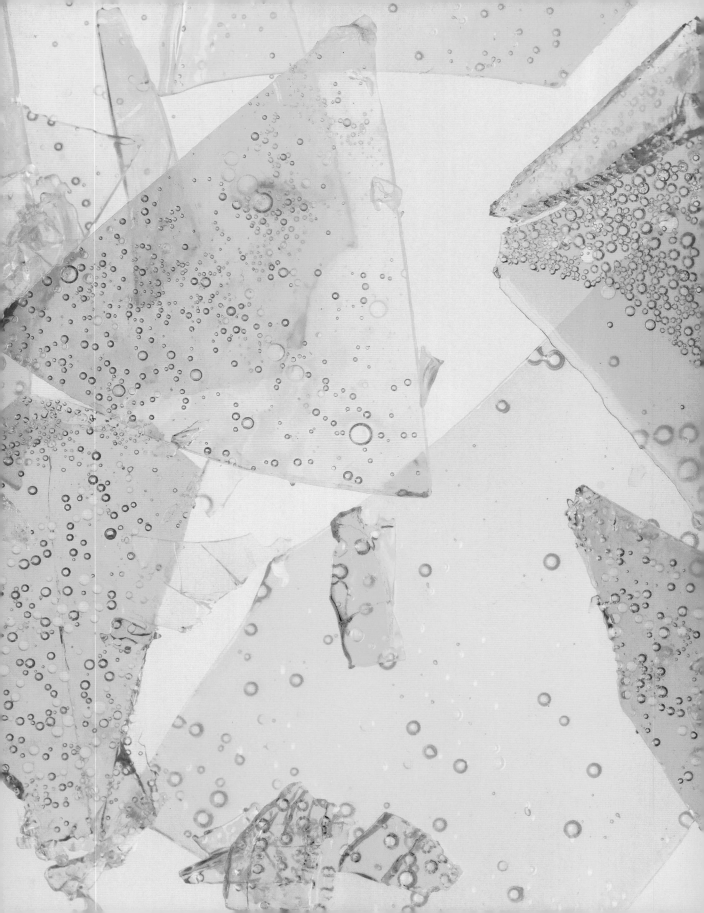